T0193757

Polar PERFECTION

Scott Kellett

authorHOUSE®

AuthorHouse™
1663 Liberty Drive
Bloomington, IN 47403
www.authorhouse.com
Phone: 1 (800) 839-8640

Published by AuthorHouse 05/07/2018

ISBN: 978-1-5462-4026-6 (sc)
ISBN: 978-1-5462-4025-9 (hc)
ISBN: 978-1-5462-4024-2 (e)

Library of Congress Control Number: 2018905205

Print information available on the last page.

UNDERSTANDING

This story of polar perfection, the story starts with me, Scott Kellett. This is how a young boy could progress to becoming a responsible adult. I wanted to write this story so that you can understand where and how any child can have a chance at a better life if you believe and work. I was adopted by my parents in 1972 by a family who were loving and caring. At an early age I was shown the morals that they would like for me to follow. My father was disabled from a mining accident and my mom was a general laborer. My parents had a strict schedule. We ate together and had family times. I think this organization had a huge influence on me and how I evolved. My sister was quiet and kind. She rarely complained. Every summer we went camping and did family things which some of my most fond memories came from. My cousins were also a part of this tight-knit family that enjoyed every time we got together.

The great thing about being young is there are no worries like adults have. The big things like paying for sports, taking time for others, or anything that occupies your time like most of our parents did at one time or another was never a care for me. This is where I believe I learned to do for others and self-sacrifice. I learned from good people, and those people were all on the same dedication towards youth. When you see people come together for a good cause, it makes you understand and believe that you can make a difference. We try to teach our children and hope they lead by a positive example that we set forth. Taking into account who gave what and respecting them for this is a strong beginning. Being a leader is not an easy thing to do; while being positive and reassuring is definitely a good start. I believe the choices a child makes are not entirely theirs. The responsible adult needs to take in account peer pressure, and help make the correct decision for the child. I have heard more parents complain that they don't understand why their child is not behaving the way they would like. I feel that peers are a huge influence in the development of their child.

Funny thing in this world, we learn to read, do math, social studies, and all academics that help us become smarter and grow, but social skills are taken for granted. The abilities of our children who we hope do right by and hope they keep on the right track. I am unaware if it was the punishment or the self-discipline that I learned the most from. I tend to lean towards the punishment. Today we spank our kids or give time-outs, but I know for certain it was the fear of being spanked that deterred me from doing wrong. These morals or sets of beliefs set forth who we will become in life. I chose to be the one who would save, rather than be saved. Not sure if it was my catholic upbringing or the good people I chose to be a part of my life.

Once I became a little older I had a great respect for law enforcement and wanted to be one of them. Growing up, my neighbor was a police officer, and I wanted to be like him. I had some law enforcement in my family. My Uncle was in the state police and my great grandfather was a county sheriff in the early 1920's. I had dreams of being a fire fighter, police officer or a soldier. In my high school years I tried to solidify this by taking classes and even completed one through the local police station. I think that learning from these leaders helped me to decide to go to college and later become a corrections officer. This discipline and 16 + years of service have helped me to grow into a positive role model and a better person.

All of these experiences in my life helped me to contribute and hopefully touch the young lives entrusted to me as I coach football, baseball and hockey. I am a huge supporter of mentors and people who support and teach younger kids. This was something that I did whenever I had the time. Any kid can have a dad, uncle or aunt. The older brothers, cousins and neighborhood kids were my heroes. My dad knew that and used to bring me to the high school football, baseball and hockey games to see them play. They were my mentors and I looked up to them. I would always tell the players I looked up to that I saw them play and how I thought how awesome they were. Each and every time they would smile and ask me if I saw something they did great on the field. The whole time I was learning the things I teach now to my teams.

The reason for understanding how I became who I am is not from all the good times or the bad, but I believe the great experiences I have had. Some of my greatest memories were watching sports with my friends and family. Some of the greatest memories were my dad and I watching the 1980 winter Olympics and beating the US hockey team VS the Russians in the "Miracle on Ice". I remember my friend Luke and me watching our first professional football and hockey games together. I can also remember my cousin Larry Lapachin and me sneaking out of church early so we could watch football at our grandpa's apartment or playing catch at Milwaukee's County Stadium before a Brewers' double header with my dad, Uncle Larry and Uncle Ray watching us. These events have assisted to make me the man who I am today.

GROWTH

The next years were a flash, the things I remember most were the great quotes my dad or coaches had. It is the lessons that I was taught and the reasoning's for those lessons that I remember most. The details of a young life with the wrong things being hammered out and the right choices praised, in hope the right choices would continue. Now as an adult I see what it was that my parents tried to instill in me, and what I can bring to those lives I touch. The person I saw most was my dad, a sports fan, who was strict with me and for good reason. I was a hot-headed, red head. Doing wrong came easy, but correcting me each and every time as my parents did was the right thing to do. As I grew a few years older, Larry and I both grew to love sports. Hockey was number one, while baseball and football were close seconds. Larry was smaller than I was, but he was just as strong and quick. We grew to push each other unknowingly, in ways that we wouldn't realize until our twenties.

The next lesson I learned was about personal hygiene. The little things mom and dad taught us were meant for nothing else, but to help us live a long and happy life. Things like brushing my teeth seemed to be a hard thing to get through my thick head, but after suffering bleeding gums and losing a tooth it sunk in. Showering was an easy lesson to learn. It seems that having to sit near someone who didn't do this gave me the ambition to do this daily. I teach these same lessons to each and every team I coach. Good hygiene and grades, positive behavior and a strong work ethic are the base for a successful life.

The ability to listen to your parents, to make hard, but right decisions, helps people to develop social skills. These skills can be developed by being a part of something bigger than they are. The individuals who are in band, sports, or any positive organization seem to make further gains in the positive aspects of their life. If you truly want kids to succeed you have to pay attention to them, talk to them and be a part of not only their life but the lives of their friends as well. All of these developments were instrumental in constructing the positive morals and great friends that I have been blessed with.

I know what I am saying seems easy, but life is such an uphill battle. I think everything depends on your heart. The stronger the heart the better things turn out when you face that uphill battle. The strength of your family, friends and your faith are all pivotal in your growth as a person. You have to buy into the principle of mentoring and being a role model. The issues that you set forth will mold what you want to build. A good base and beliefs, religious or not, will contribute to what you want for your child.

When your child's growth is your main concern (which it should be), you should create an atmosphere that mirrors what you want for your child. If you want to try to steer them in a direction of football let's say, you should adapt to that concept and make a great effort to conform to that idea. For example, if your nephew is a football player you should make an effort to see him play and be a part of that experience. Your child will see this and naturally want to be a part of that experience as well. You have to go to the games, watch games on TV and actually play with your kid whether you are athletic or not. Mom may not be able to throw a perfect spiral, but attempting to do it will teach so much more to her child. Growth is not always accomplished by watching, but can be accomplished by participation, which is more important than any other method in my opinion.

The last step in growth is positive reinforcement. To help your child grow it is not sufficient enough just to say "good job." A pat on the back, hug or some type of physical contact is a great way to get a positive response by your child. Another thing that is very important is follow up. Follow up can be done at the dinner table. Ask your child what they did in school, at their practice or what they did with their friends that day, as this will give them a feeling of worth. The feeling of worth is what helps some kids do positive things. These positive feelings will grow like a tree and will make a wonderful base for great things in life to follow.

Taking the importance of school and your studies in the idealism of growth is very important in the growth of your child. I never got good grades. I'm not sure why I didn't, but my parents took me out of hockey for a year for not getting grades that they wanted me to have. As a coach, I try to support parents by reiterating the importance of having good grades. I often talk to the players and student coaches about school. I show them that I care, and they always respond to my positive words with smiles. I do not hold back that I didn't get the best grades, and I want them to get better so they can get a better job than I have.

THE EARLY YEARS

Everything has an effect on life - positively and negativity. Some choose to ignore the positive and I have no idea why that is, but for me the choice was an easy one. I always felt that being adopted and the gift of life was so precious that anything should be done to preserve it, cherish it and bring happiness to that child. I remember being a small boy with my best friend and Cousin Larry. We were competitive and as close to brothers as any could be. I remember being three or four years old and Larry and I racing in the yard, playing whiffleball, tackle football or anything that we could do to keep out of our parent's hair.

A big part of my childhood was the family birthday parties. Having such a close family made for great birthday parties with competitive games and great food. Learning about losing didn't come easy. Larry and I grew closer as friends and competitors to the end. All of my cousins would play baseball or other kid games with everyone, and it seemed no-one did anything on their own. Our family was close and that has never changed.

In 1977 I was 5 years old. It was a very good year. My sister Kellie was born along with other great surprises like going to kindergarten, t-ball and hockey. I loved competition. Winning was a great feeling and losing sucked. I loved learning to do all the advanced things, from throwing a spiral to placing your fingers correctly to throw a curve. The older kids in the neighborhood taught me a lot without even knowing it. To the older kids I was a 5 year old they could get to do anything for them, and to me they were gods and mentors, always teaching me without knowing what they were doing.

I remember going to the Colonial Building to play hockey for the first time. I was nervous, but it helped that my dad, Uncle Larry and Little Larry all went to the rink with me. The excitement of touching the ice was quickly extinguished by the unbalanced blades and the routine falling. After a few tears and once the pain wore off, my cousin and I would pull ourselves up off the ice and try to skate all over again. After a few skating lessons, I was hooked and attempted to get on the ice every chance I could. The world had a new look with new opportunities. I was the only hockey player in my neighborhood. I remember spending hours outside shooting pucks at the snow bank.

Winter had a whole new look since I was introduced to the great sport of hockey. I went from building snow forts to sniping the snow bank. I couldn't wait to go to practice to see my coaches and the high school students whom I looked up to for encouragement and knowledge. The longer the season, the faster I felt on my skates. The games were a chance to show mom and dad how much I improved and I tried to make my coaches proud. I didn't know I was getting better, I just knew I was having fun and it was the best feeling in the world. My cousin and I would play every chance we were together, whether it was inside the house or outside in the driveway. I was so eager to play that my father and other dads flooded a field near our house in the winter, so we could skate whenever we wanted.

The really cool thing about hockey compared to others was that our team had kids from other schools, and even other local towns. Some of the friendships I have today were made in those early years. I was apprehensive about meeting and playing with kids from other towns at first because it wasn't familiar to me. Having simple conversations on the ice with the kids helped to get rid of any anxiety that I had after a just few practices. By the end of the season they were my friends and that would never change. After the season I always missed my new friends and my parents encouraged me to have many sleepovers with my new friends to keep those bonds.

At the beginning of each season to following the first one, was an uncoordinated beginning which developed to a graceful ending. Every year had a lesson to teach and I was a student of the game. Many visions come to me of the early years, none of which are bad ones. Year after year my friends would return and sometimes I'd make new friends who would sign up and play the season with us. I met friends like Luke, who in later years would remain my best friend and would name me his son's Godfather. Often when I am coaching kids, I wonder if they are going to have the great experiences that I have had.

Some lessons are hard to take, but are a must in the growth and development. My early learning lessons were taking away my hockey stick and grounding me to my room. I was a stubborn red head and I thought if I didn't budge then mom and dad would. I was wrong. Each and every time I would apologize, sometimes crying to my parents asking for forgiveness for what I had done wrong. I give my parents a ton of credit, because sometimes I was a little devil and deserved to be punished. This helped me to understand right from wrong, forgiveness, and even humility. If I were to ever be caught in a lie I would be shown mercy if I were to tell the truth. This taught me that good things can happen if you were to have those humbling attributes.

The lesson I remember best and probably the hardest one I have ever had to learn was when my parents decided to take me out of hockey because my grades were horrible. It was my first peewee year. I was in fifth grade and I didn't have the respect or the attention for school that I should have. My parents sat me down in the kitchen after they looked at my report card and told me they decided to take me out of hockey until my grades improved. I was devastated. I ran to my room and cried. I couldn't believe what was happening and thought the world was coming to an end.

I reached a bitter anger towards my teacher and deep down I blamed her for what had happened. I didn't realize the responsibility was that of my own to get my homework done and the blame was all mine. After a week or so my dad brought me to Larry's hockey game. He made me sit and watch. I sat suffering because I missed playing. The next day at school I became so furious with my teacher for taking my beloved sport away that I did something dumb. I went home after school and got an egg. I slowly crept to a snow bank and threw the egg at the teacher's car. I hit the car and watched the yolk go down her front windshield. I initially felt like I had redeemed myself in some juvenile way, but soon I felt guilty and the next day I told my parents. My parents went to school with me and I told the principal and the teacher what I had done. After some initial scolding, then some respectful appreciation for my honesty, I was sent out with a sponge and a bucket to clean the egg off her car. I learned a valuable lesson about honesty and doing wrong. I was grounded for what I had done, but not as severe since I told the truth.

My grades improved, and so did my attitude. My parents let me return to play hockey later that year, and I rewarded them with hard work and less headaches. I grew to become a harder, more focused worker after that. The next summer I became a focused baseball player by playing catch or hitting whenever I could. At eleven years old I had a great summer playing little league. I felt I had done a fantastic job pitching for my team. When time came for all-star selections I came up short and I didn't understand why. Parent coaches had put their kids on the all-star team before others that deserved it even more than I did, in my opinion. This was my first experience with politics, and I hated it as much then as I do now.

The winter of 1984 brought more eye openers. I tried out for the Pee Wee A team. Again I gave all I had and felt I did a pretty good job, only to find out that again I came up short to other players I knew were inferior to me and the other good players that were not chosen. I felt as if I didn't give a good enough effort and that I wasn't good enough. My dad gave me his speech, "There is always going to be somebody better, faster, and stronger." For years I thought about this and it drove me nuts. I felt as if I could never be the best in his eyes. I used this as motivation, and I was going to show the old man that I was the best. I started to lift weights and practice harder. The idea of taking second place was not in my vocabulary. After watching those mentors lift weights, I took what I learned from them and worked out hard. Sports came a little easier to me after using a weight program.

Competition was already instilled in me, and I naturally gave one hundred percent effort. The practice of pitching, shooting and running all started to come together for me. The next summer I played my last spring of little league for Ironwood Little League. I was one of the oldest in the league and did pretty well. I could throw really well, but I couldn't hit the ball if it were on a tee. That year I was chosen for the All-star team and pretty much only played when I was pitching. When I pitched I was effective, I struck out the last 3 batters of our district championship game. Our team ended up losing in the finals of the Upper Peninsula of Michigan championship, but we did an excellent job.

The next tournament, which was a local one in Hurley, Wisconsin, was a great lesson to learn. The team I was on was split into two groups called All-star 1 and All-star 2. The idea was that the best players were on All-star 1 and the secondary players were put on All-star 2. I was on the All-star 1 team and can't remember if our team wasn't prepared or we just got outplayed. The moral of the story is we got our butts handed to us by a group of kids who thought they should have been on my All-star1 team. I felt deep down that we were going to lose, but I didn't care. My best friends were on that other team, and they performed great. My cousin Larry had a couple of hits and scored some runs, and Jamie, my friend, was on the mound. Jamie pitched a gem throwing knuckleballs that we couldn't hit. Even though I loved to compete, I learned that being a sportsman is very important and the growth of sportsmanship is invaluable.

JUNIOR HIGH

Being in high school seemed to be a big deal for my parents, but I was as nervous as I have ever felt. Walking into that big school was an experience I would never forget. The first day of school we had a meeting for any 7th or 8th grade player that wanted to play football. I watched football for years with my family and looked forward to playing. We didn't have any pop warner football or pee wee football. I went out for junior high football in both of my junior high years (7th & 8TH grade). I started to learn about the physical aspect of contact sports. I also learned about how nutrition plays a really big part in performance in sports. I learned for the first time that if my grades were not where the school wanted I couldn't play. The seventh grade year got off on the right foot, playing football with my buddies and lifting weights in the high school weight room. Life was good and it was only going to get better.

After football season came hockey. Club hockey did not have the same requirements with grades and playing but I knew that if I didn't get good grades my parents would take me out of hockey. It seemed that the contact in football along with the discipline had made me a better overall player. The Pee Wee season had checking and I was a lot better at it because of football. My speed was much improved as well as my strength. I had a blast with all of my hockey buddies and the season was a blast.

Track and field came after hockey in the spring. I tried everything from pole vault to shot put. I liked doing shot put and the 400 meter dash. I wasn't very fast compared to the kids on my team, but I could compete with the shot put. This fun new experience helped to develop team building, because, even though you were competing as an individual you meant something to your team. Winning your event would give your team points, and the team with the most points won. The speed training and weight lifting was a crucial point in my learning about sport injuries and how to prevent them.

During the last part of my first year of Junior high school, I was playing Babe Ruth baseball. I really liked playing baseball, but it wasn't as meaningful as it was in little league. I think that for the most part I went through the motions so I could stay in shape for football and hockey. I even think that I was doing it more because my father really liked watching baseball.

My eighth grade year the classes got harder for me so my grades did slip a little, but I always did well enough to play. I remember sitting down with my mom and I asked her, "What is worth more? Good common sense or good grades?" I asked this because being in high school I saw that kids were doing drugs, drinking and skipping school. I knew that playing sports in high school could keep you on track. You can't play if your grades slip, get in trouble or violate the code of conduct. Even though I was around the pressures that are introduced in high school, I knew what the consequences were for violating those rules. I watched as some kids were caught smoking, drinking, or other violations and they were punished by suspensions from athletics. At the end of my eighth grade year there was a meeting I attended that would change my life. The meeting was for hockey players who were interested in high school hockey. The meeting was about fundraising and trying to get enough capital to start a team. There was going to be the first ever Ironwood high school hockey team, and it was great news.

5

HIGH SCHOOL

One of the biggest changes in my life was the summer of 1987. I had things to do every day. If I wasn't busy lifting weights, I was busy doing something else. It seemed like there was always something to do, and I don't remember sitting home at all. Football started in August. My freshman year was a whole new ball game. We started the season out with two practices a day at football camp. I am not sure, but the soreness from the non-stop exercising was more pain than I ever have had in my young life. I thought I was in shape, but I learned a lesson yet again - you can always work harder. Football was fun, but I couldn't stop thinking about trying out for the high school hockey team.

After a successful football season came what I have been training for, the tryout for the high school hockey team. The try out was an organized group of skills and drills. I know that I gave all I had on every drill, and even though I wasn't the fastest, I never quit. My cousin Larry was doing very well and I hoped just to keep up. We gave each other words of encouragement every break that we had. Larry and I pushed our physical limits on each drill. We gave an effort that didn't go unnoticed. After the try out we were picked to play varsity hockey for Ironwood high school. Four freshmen made the team and the coach made it known that we were not there to watch but to participate in each and every game.

I cannot even begin to explain the joy that I experienced when stepping on the ice for the first time. It was like the nervousness of Christmas morning. I felt like I had something to prove. A part of me still didn't feel

14

a part of the team because I had never made a tryout for anything. The challenges that were facing Larry and I were just beginning.

Unknowingly, we were hated by our own team members because a few of the senior buddies were cut from the team. It took no time at all to feel unwelcome. Some of the drills that the team did were an excuse to attempt to hurt us in one way or another. I would be lying if I told you that I hadn't thought of quitting. The season had steady moments where I looked over my shoulder, nervous of these huge juniors and seniors hunting us. After a month or so, the coach became aware of these bad intentions and dealt with it and punished them. My coach understood what was happening and didn't have to say a word to me, his actions showed his support. About half way through the season my coach told me that he picked me because he sees potential and a lot of heart. I tried to utilize this in my own coaching technique by making the kids feel worthwhile. I believe the health of a player's mind is just as important as their body.

After a successful first season of high school hockey, I rolled right into high school track. Nothing out of the ordinary happened with the exception of being in awe of some of the talented people that would compete in their individual sports. Over the next year, I played my last year of Babe Ruth and kept on lifting weights until my sophomore year. I played football for the junior varsity team until hockey began. The second hockey season was a very good year. We were young, but a feisty group of players. I made a promise that I would never treat anyone like we were treated that freshman year. I think the most valuable lesson I learned from that was to respect others and treat everyone like you would like to be treated.

My junior year of athletics I became focused in a way that would supersede anything else that was going on. My first varsity football team had a group of really great players. We were like family, and I learned quickly that injuries are part of sports and you have to adjust. Sometimes adjusting is not something you would like to do, but it is necessary for the good of the team. The sacrifice is a decision by the coach to place a team mate or yourself into a position that you are not accustom to, but because it will make the team better.

Hockey season came quickly, and I was raring and ready. Our team was primarily made of juniors, and we were hungry to win. Our team was very young but we were talented. My passion for hockey was becoming more and more. The team was like family just like our football team. Our coaches had done a good job of keeping the team together and making sure we had the same desire that they had. We had an excellent season but came up short at the end with a heartbreaking loss.

I think the blur of track and high school baseball was caused by me not being a difference maker just a role player on those teams. I have never forgotten how great it was to cheer and be a good team mate. I felt that I was best at supporting the team and always giving heartfelt words to those who were upset by a poor performance. I try to use these attributes to my coaching.

My senior year I started on a football team with great expectations. The team did excellent posting a 6-3 record and just narrowly missing the playoffs. I always took the time to talk to the neighbor kids who would talk to me about my performance. I remembered what it was like to look up to someone, and now I was that someone. It made me feel good that I could share these experiences and try to mentor these kids so they would play sports too. I would help anyone who would ask, from playing catch with a kid in the neighborhood to teaching the kids how to throw a spiral. I know that some parents really appreciated what I did, but for me it was natural to help.

Playing in front of the home crowd was the best feeling as a player I ever felt. The fans, mostly high school kids, were rowdy and loud. The more we hit the louder and more out of control they became. This was the only time that I can remember where students from all surrounding towns got along and cheered together. I loved to hit. My team mates loved to hit as well, and they did so with thunderous applause. Our football season was a great success but missing the playoffs was a great disappointment.

My last season of high school hockey was a blast. I practiced and played my heart out. I cherished each and every moment on the ice, I knew that this was my last season and I didn't want to live with any regrets. My favorite part of hockey was checking. I sometimes felt like a goon and maybe with good reason. I wish I could have been able to stickhandle like some of the better players or snipe the top shelf, but hitting helped our team win. Even though I was bumped and bruised from sacrificing my body any way I could, I wanted to win more than anything. We had a group of talented "Yoopers" that fought every battle and never quit. (Yoopers are what we call people that live in Michigan's Upper Peninsula.)

Our high school team was called the Red Devils, and we were an unstoppable force when we wanted to be. Larry and Luke could score and the defense was tough and gritty. I always knew that working out and giving one hundred percent would pay off in one way or another. My God given attributes were my speed and strength, and I used them to the best of my ability. I used my body any way I could to help my team win. I blocked shots and checked every chance I could. My other team mates had just as good, if not better, attributes. The team was very sacrificial, what you would want out of any team. The team was very experienced with most of the team being seniors. This team was big, fast, and skilled what you would want for a team to develop into a championship caliber team.

Having a power house team is a great feeling to have. You know any of your team mates has the potential of winning any game. At the beginning of the season I knew we had what it took. All of the team members got along great, and still do. As far as a team goes it was probably the tightest knit group of guys I have been affiliated with. We were feared, not only for our great goal scorers, but for our tough defense that would punish you. I took the things I learned those four years and kept them close to my heart. I use everything I have learned and directed it to a philosophy for winning.

Our team had all of the components to have a state championship team. The team had heart, dedication, and hardworking players and coaches. So what went wrong? Injuries, overconfidence, and lack of preparation were all factors in this dream season's demise. One reason we did poorly was because we had a bunch of injuries that never seemed to end. The last, and I think the biggest reason for our self-demise, was overconfidence. In the newspaper we were ranked in the Michigan top 10 teams. I think this gave us a cockiness that started our downward spiral.

The negative things I learned the most from my senior season I take with a heavy heart and try to avoid the failures that I experienced with my new team. I am not sure if the breakdowns were on a few individuals or the team as a whole. The breakdowns in discipline that I believe killed us were drinking, smoking, drugs, and poor preparation. I blame some of this on myself for not taking the initiative to intervene and put some players in check. I failed to be a leader; this would haunt me for years to come. My senior season which was filled with hopes and dreams fell into a sea of disappointment. My goals for my teams to win a state championship had failed.

I was taught at one of my coaching clinics that you should take drills, positive attitudes, and any other great coaching techniques from other coaches. I often thought of the great coaches and what they meant to me in my playing days. When I was starting sports in 1977, I remember a coach I had that helped me to learn to skate. Warren was his name and he was a very good coach. The student coaches that helped us to skate, I really looked up to them, and my dad used to take me to their games at the old Colonial skating rink. The Colonial was an old building that had no zamboni. We were the zamboni's. Each player had to take a scraper and scrape the ice, so the fathers could flood the rink for the next day.

With each year of playing, I remember each coach and how I was affected by their teachings. Joe, Bill and my dad donated their time and energy for each of us kids. My father and Joe had an agreement that they would not coach their own kids, and it worked perfectly. This was an agreement years later that I would make with Adam and his kids. There are other coaches that really need to be mentioned because their great leadership and awesome motivation that still affect me to this day. Tom was one of the greatest coaches I have ever had. Tom was positive, assertive, and most of all caring. Tom was and always will be a great mentor for each and every player that had the privilege to play for him. He was a great teacher in school as well. He showed great energy by coaching more than one sport. His positive assertiveness helped to motivate and bring each and every one of us to a higher level of play. As a freshman, to have a coach like that was the one of the biggest reasons to succeed.

Tom was my high school hockey coach. Tom was a visionary. Many of the parents did not agree with his views. I look at things now and think back to the cuts that were made off the varsity hockey team and think what was he thinking. Tom took an enormous amount of complaints for taking four freshmen over two seniors and three juniors which is understandable. Tom must have seen the potential in each and every one of us. We worked hard every day - each of us, Scott, Chris, Larry, and me. Mr. Blooming's assistant, Dave, was just as much a great coach as Tom was. Dave showed that he believed in us unconditionally as well. In the future it would show that their visions and beliefs were right on. The Red Devils hockey team was one of the toughest in the state, and it showed with our rankings in the state polls. I think what I take most from Tom and Dave is the faith in those who can develop and to see what each player has to give to their team.

Dave is the last person I would like to mention, even though there were other coaches who affected me. Dave was my varsity football coach, and he was also my track coach as well. Dave was a great motivator and a smart coach. He played football for Central Michigan University, and it seemed he tried to push everyone to that same level of play. I was mentored during my weight training by Dave and other teammates as well. I learned to work hard to get what I had coming. I did not start my junior year. I took for granted that I would start because I thought I was better than some of the other players. I had worked out in the weight room all summer and was as strong as I had ever been, but I needed to keep working hard and get my nose to the grindstone.

Luke started at outside linebacker but got sick before our first big game of the season. I got to start and I never looked back. I learned that taking my chances and putting it all on the line for my team would pay off. Dave was a great motivator and I found that my energy was higher than it has ever been. I believed Dave would lead us to the next level of play. Every player believed in him. Each of us would have walked through fire for him. He sold his ideas to us and we in return succeeded in every aspect of the game.

Learning about life and each sport made me understand the importance of the finer things. I learned that no player is a lost cause no matter what the views of others and believe in them. I learned to help motivate players to assist them to play at another level. I learned that each player needs to be accountable and needs to be shown how to bring their own level of play to where a coach knows it can be. I saw that even the underdog can make a statement to help their team and teammates reach the next level. I learned that a coaches' positive energy can affect players in a positive way to help them get through the tough times. I saw that being organized is a way to be utterly flawless in assisting your team to make greater gains. I learned that making sacrifices through dedication, time, and caring will not only make great players but great people as well. These things were something I talked about with some of my old teammates trying to get a feel of how our success was brought about and how we could bring that to our teams.

6

ADULTHOOD

After high school I felt something was missing. Some of my old buddies would get together and play tackle football, baseball, and hockey every chance we could trying to relive the glory days. College was the main concern to give me a chance at a better life. I worked weekends at a hotel resort to pay my bills and to give me some extra money to play. One of my college teachers was asking me about hockey and if I would help her husband coach. I thought it was intriguing to coach rather than play. So I agreed to help him out. USA hockey mandates that every coach take a coaching class. I went to the class and started to coach my first hockey team.

The age was 9-10 (squirts) and I remember being so nervous. I didn't know any of these kids. I was scared I would stink as a coach and that the kids would think I was an idiot. Before taking the ice for the first time I went into the locker room and gave the kids a speech. I said," Hello my name is Scott Kellett, and I will be your coach this season. I will give you one hundred percent, and I expect the same in return. I want you all to learn as much as possible and have fun. Put your helmets on and hit the ice." The nerves went away and I felt a lot better about what I was going to do. One of the other coaches asked, "What's your plan?" I responded, "Skate them until they pass out." I looked back at the coach and smiled at him. Of course I only skated them lightly and did a bunch of drills to develop the kids' skills.

I always made some sort of sacrifice to make every practice and most games. My boss was cool with bending my schedule, and I rewarded him with working as hard as I could. I noticed every player and got to know each individual rather quickly. I found that names of the players came quickly to me. I noticed the hockey skills that were lacking and how to improve them with drills and skating techniques. At this point of my coaching career I was starting to take notes on players and where they improved and how to keep them on track. I always tried to communicate with each player and give corrective criticism on their skills. I would give positive reinforcement right at the end of practices so that would be the last thing they would hear at the end of practice.

I made a lot of mistakes with this first coaching experience. The hardest part of being a coach is trying to be fair all the time. In someone else's eyes their way or their opinion is the correct one. I was a very young man, 19 years old, and I was trying to please all the parents and the board members as well. Other parents that I knew were unbiased, and I looked to them for advice. The one thing I learned growing up was to ask for help and don't feel bad about doing it. The search for knowledge and wisdom is something I wanted to better myself at, as well as others.

I can remember the players who had difficulty doing a crossover for the first time. I would get down on my knees and with my hands on their feet show them how one foot crossed over the other. Our goalie was raw but gave 100% every practice. The team had a raw talent. The biggest thing they had going for them is they had fun each and every day. They never won and they never lost.

My biggest mistake I made early on in my coaching career was getting over excited. When my heart would start pumping and my adrenaline was at its peak, I would lose my mind on the bench. To get excited is one thing, but to let your emotions take control is another. I was a big yeller at the start and I still am when it comes to certain situations. I would yell about every little call I felt didn't go our team's way. I saw that if affected the team in a negative way, and on a rare occasion it motivated some of the players. I didn't mean to belittle the referees but only to make them aware in a loud tone.

I didn't realize until after a mistake was made of what damage you can do with the tone of a voice. On occasion when I was yelling and trying to motivate some of the players they would respond in a negative way. Some players cannot take any loudness what so ever. I saw some good players shut down towards me and my loud antics. I was so young myself and thought I knew more than I did. I learned from my many mistakes to help a player become a better player. As for some of the players the negative response affects the team not only the player. These mistakes would help me to further myself, not only as a coach, but as a better person as well.

Selfish players can self destroy a team. Players that have been selfish can affect the other players' growth. A player who refuses to pass and only shoot becomes a one dimensional player. The team make up becomes hostile as players refuse to pass to the selfish player. Parents start to have their opinions shown by their children's attitude. I didn't recognize these destructive things that could happen to a team until they unfolded on my own.

Coaching is probably one of the most challenging things I have done in my life. The challenges that I faced that first season developed my temper, feelings towards others, and my communication with all ages. I always went and apologized to the players whose feelings I would hurt soon after making the mistake. That is the thing about coaching, it is an exploration of what you can and can't say to a player. Players are sensitive, and I didn't take that into account in some of my speeches to an individual or a team. I found that some players need you to be brutally honest and some need to be given nothing but positive reaffirmation. It is difficult to feel out what triggers a player's capability, but I do know this, they all have a trigger to get a better game out of them.

With that first season I learned what was appropriate and what wasn't. The parents were very helpful and it was a great experience. I found that talking to players and getting assistance from their parents was very helpful. I wanted to teach the players that there were no secrets on that team or from the parents. The open line of communication was invaluable to me as a rookie coach. The pressures of making mistakes were less, than I expected which made my experience easier. The players and coaches that I interacted with are still my friends.

I took from that first season a heart of a winner. The team had more heart than any team I have ever been a part of. I consider this team the best lesson I could have had in my life. Winning didn't matter but their progress on the ice did. They all cared about it and showed it by their steady improvement. A few years later the team won the 1st state championships.

7

PROFESSIONAL LIFE

The season was over too soon over; I went to work for the Michigan Department of Corrections. With this new experience, my life away from home for the first time was beginning. My parents were very excited about me getting hired, and I was twice as nervous. I wasn't sure if I could do it - being away from home and having no friends or family with me, but I believed I was ready for the responsibility of being on my own. Going to the academy seemed to be a good idea at first, but coming from a little town like Ironwood and going to Lansing was like climbing Mount Everest. You look from the outside and think it is no big deal and then you feel how small you are.

The academy was surrounded by crime ridden streets, constant sirens, and unfriendly faces everywhere. I saw the world as it was portrayed on the six o'clock news. In my hometown, if your car broke down someone would stop and help you out. In the big city no one seems to smile or say hi in a friendly manner. I didn't think that this line of work was for me. My first day of the academy was filled with signing of papers and new job routines. The second day is one I will never forget. I had gone into a world of hate and discontent. I grew up in a family that was loving and kind; both were signs of weakness that would shorten ones career in the field I chose. The Department was very specific about what they want you to do as an employee and what you will do.

I quickly found out that the application of this negative environment would be a mainstay in my professional life. The good thing is the department is filled with good people in a negative environment. It takes some people a long time to avoid the negativity and not duplicate it. And it took me years to learn to be myself. I was fortunate to have good hearted people to work with. This job is not for the faint of heart. The inmates have nothing to do but watch and study you and use anything they can to give them what they want. I learned from great people how to balance the negativity and not bring it into my personal life. The divorce rate within the employees of the Department of Corrections speaks for itself. It wasn't an easy transition to leave work behind when I lived in a strange place with no friends.

Luke would come and visit me on occasion. I mostly went home on my days off to hang out with my old friends and bring some normalcy to my life. For the three years I was working in Manistique it was crucial to have exposure with people that were as positive and supportive as the co-workers that I was blessed to have. I was very lonely living there without my family. I met some really good friends there and co-workers who I think about every day. The people I worked with taught me how to interact with inmates in a positive manner. Corrections is unique in that the personalities you work with, employee and offender, can affect your professional and personal life. I learned how difficult this was not having a social life and most of your personal contact came at work. It was quickly corrected with social interaction of non-corrections people that some of my conversational tactics were not acceptable.

I learned some social skills that normal people do not find acceptable. Some of these skills are total honesty, direct and to the point, and firm and fair justifications. When I first came in contact with the inmate population, I learned to correct any mistake by being honest. I always correct the problem by apologizing for my mistake and move on. Many people do not forgive mistakes lightly, but I try to forget them as fast as they are made. Not holding grudges is a very hard thing to do but it is necessary. Honesty is something that people will respect and appreciate. I not only learn this valuable lesson, but I try to teach it as much as possible.

A lesson I learned is communication should be direct and to the point. Trying not to hurt someone's feelings is very difficult. I believe that being honest at all times is a great way to become a leader. I found out that when using any type of punishment, I would have to be honest and to the point of what and why. The punishment you give must be firm and fair. It is difficult, but using your discretion is always a good way to keep decisions fair. Punishment is a tool to help enforce discipline. I acknowledged when I made a mistake there was always a price to pay. At work I would use whatever punishment fit the infraction and dealt with it. I learned that in no matter what discipline you are inflicting, you must give an explanation of why and how.

Decision making was one of the last things I learned. Making good decisions is hard. There is someone who will always disagree and not understand why that particular decision was made. When working in a corrections environment, the decisions you make are always under scrutiny. I learned that being honest and doing your best is all you can do. The decisions you make sometimes have to be quick and without thought. You have to take all the learning experiences that life has to offer. At work you learn that to make a decision, right or wrong, it is appreciated by both sides. I have taken this and use this in my everyday life.

HOME

After living in Manistique for three years, I transferred to a prison back home and moved back to Ironwood. I was just content living each day as simply as possible. I worked afternoon shift and had little or no responsibility. Every day had no meaning, and it seemed I was happy with a routine of bar hopping, lifting weights and failed relationships. I was haunted by words I told a girlfriend when I was in high school. I dated a girl named Jo Ann, she is a nice girl and we are friends to this day. But what I told her reminds me of the life that I wanted to live. After a lengthy discussion of being adopted and life, I told Jo Ann "I want to do something with this life that was given to me." I explained to Jo Ann that making the right decision, like being a designated driver, would define who I would become.

I was grateful that my parents were always honest about me being adopted. I always have been honest with my friends about this as my parents were to me. If you are to think that it meant nothing to be adopted you are dead wrong. My parents always explained to me that being adopted is being chosen. I think that helps some of the outcome of my decisions. I don't drink, do drugs, or use tobacco, and I felt that having a clean train of thought would always keep me on the right path. I also know that leading by example is the number one way to teach future leaders the good qualities they should posses as well.

I always have loved having kids around, whether it was mentoring or playing some game with them. I think as a society we need to keep on a positive track and do our best to keep on it. Some of the focus in my life hasn't really strayed too far from trying to keep positive. When it comes to the kids I have coached, I have used what I learned throughout my adulthood to notice possible problems with the kids and attempt to intervene. I have coached kids who have been physically abused by their parents, amongst other things. I have always been very direct. In doing this there are only two things that can happen. The first is some people appreciate this directness and are reciprocal in nature. The second is some people are so offended by being honest and direct that it causes more problems in the future. If you have the best interest in mind, and are pure in spirit, I believe you will install a great base for the kids to learn from.

I feel that a simple compliment is not out of line. Telling someone good job or well done can change their opinion of you and the dynamics of your relationship. The positive effect of a smile can change not only their day but your own as well.

I remember from a movie a man says," Son are you proud of the things you have done with this life? If not you had better get it right." Sayings and other quotes from movies or iconic figures helps form for a relation to which most can understand. I often use movies as a motivation to get a point through to the players. For the development and the growth of each individual player requires great thought and an understanding of the individual. The fact of the matter is what happened in my youth and those coaches and mentors who impacted me most did so by understanding me. I try to use this by remembering that I thought my parents were old and didn't understand anything about life. But on the contrary the growth and development starts with them.

I believe that family is the most important thing in every individual's life. Sports are filler between what is really important. The thing to remember is that those who are on your team are your family at that particular time. The rink or ball field is your home, and it should be cherished as such. My dad once told me when I was younger, "friends may come and go, but family is forever." I look back at photos and all the great memories that I had with my friends and family. I think about how I hope to help my hockey kids experience the awesome life I have had. I always think about that and how each player can have "their" moment. After I moved back home, I wanted to contribute in some way. I wasn't sure how, but I was confident I was going to do something positive and give back what was given to me. I wanted to show how I have learned the positive things I could install into our community.

27

THE VOID

After moving back home to Ironwood, I was twenty-five years old, and I wanted to start to get my life on track. I had a plan to get on with some type of normalcy. My main focus wasn't anything other than settling down, buy a house and work until I retire. It was a little boring. Most of the people I worked with had kids that were in some type of school sports or other daily activities. I wanted that too. The white picket fence, kids, nice car, and the whole shebang. The fact of life is some things don't turn out the way that you would like. I tried the best I could to have the American dream, but it wouldn't happen the way I had planned.

I bought a house and remodeled it the best I could. It was a good beginning to the way I was trying to set up my life and live happily. I put a lot of time and money into my house, as I do my own life. I wasn't sure if the dedication to complete the house was because of my inner need to succeed or because I was afraid it wouldn't get done. From the first nail to the last coat of paint, everything that was cherished and appreciated. My carpentry skills are not as good as you might think, in fact they are mediocre at best. I did the best I could and learned that perfection doesn't come as easy as some make it out.

My plan of my life was taking form. I was happy with what I had, but I wanted more. I wanted kids. Being adopted gave me an appreciation of what it meant to be a parent. I wanted children to help complete my life and give my parents something to look for. After living a disciplined life through my parents and my mentors, I knew that I could be an excellent

Father. I saw the great parents my friends had become spending time with friends and their father did fill the void of not having children for a while, but there was something missing. I didn't know what it was, but I was searching.

Working on afternoon shift was hard on having a normal life. You wait all day long to go to work, then get home late at night with nothing opened other than the bars. That is exactly what I did. I found great friends at the bar. My buddy Brian owned a bar. I met Brian as soon as I moved back to town. There was a big group of us that hung out there and became great friends. We all had some sort of an athletic background, so naturally we played any sports we could outside of the bar. We actually had a pretty decent softball team that kept together for a few years and also played flag football. Each and every friend got along great with one another, and we were not just bar buddies but friends for life.

After a few years of the same routine, I noticed a little sadness in myself. It wasn't that my friends or family wasn't enough. My failed relationships had worn on me a little bit, but it wasn't loneliness that was making me sad. It was the void I had in my heart that wasn't filling. I did some soul searching at our family's cottage at Little Girls Point on beautiful Lake Superior. It was a place that since I was a young boy I could go and be at peace. It was a party place for my buddies and a meeting place for our family. I have enjoyed the sunsets and the vicious storms each beautiful in its own way. Helping me to sleep and keep at peace. I would play music on the radio at night and start a fire in the fireplace and sit until late at night. This is one of the most enjoyable things of my life. This was my sanctuary. My own private getaway.

The best decisions I ever made were done after I thought them through at the cottage. It seems the relaxed and tranquil environment was perfect to thinking things through. I knew two basic things: a change was needed and I was the only one who could change it. I have always found that happiness was not just found, but created by positive people whom I care about. The notion I came up with was working in the negative environment day in and day out for a better than a third of my life was killing me as a person. My ability to care about the little things were gone, concern and other feelings were non-existent. I was an unemotional zombie who felt nothing for anyone.

I would put on a fake smile and kept up with my routine of working, lifting weights, and doing what I could do to get through the day. I was in my early thirties wondering when retirement would come to change this empty existence I had made for myself. The world was not appealing to me anymore, I wasn't interested in anything. I craved something to fill me up with the joy I once felt when I was younger. I didn't want to go to any social events. I didn't want to do anything but pay my bills and watch TV. But I always found some time to look at my old scrap books and remember the roar of the crowd. I deep down missed hockey.

My friends knew something was off because I was not going to the bar, local sporting events, or family gatherings anymore. I was socially dead. I did love to be social at one time, but somewhere along the way I became detached emotionally to the world. I accepted the fact that this was my life, and I was going to just cruise through it the best that I could. I just hoped that a change would force me out of this funk and get my pathetic excuse for a life going in the positive direction that I wanted.

A FRESH START

The positive of this time in my life, which I believe was the start to get me back on track to which I really am, was Dan "Boone". He was a good friend and team mate from high school that approached me about coaching. Boone is a great guy and always was one of my mentors early on in life. I had seen a once great football team that I was a part of go astray years later. I found out that Boone was coaching and asked if I would help in some way. I figured that this was a great opportunity to lift weights again and get back in shape. I told Boone I would open the weight room and give my all to help these kids with their lifting and cardio. Boone was more than happy to have any help to get the football program up and running again.

As always when I start a project I give one hundred ten percent. No excuses. I started out with five players lifting from grades 7-12, and by the end of the summer there were around thirty kids participating in lifting and running. I do not take credit for this, but give the credit to Boone. He got the kids to believe in his philosophy. This was the first hand experience I needed to be a part of. After lifting with the kids, I grew attached to their hard work and great attitudes I forgot about. I saw the drive grow in each individual player, into a well-oiled machine ready to hit the gridiron. I think the thing I liked most was the simple problems of high school kids. Trivial and enormous at the same time. I had become that mentor to some of these players that my old mentors were to me.

The harmony and the feeling I got helping these kids grow as people and as athletes was a great beginning to a winning combination. I am not sure where the place in life is for people who hate to see the positive and are compelled to be negative and bring themselves down, but they always seem to surface. Some of the adults would concentrate on the negative these kids had in their lives. These people would want to take football or any other happiness these kids could find and take it for their own satisfaction. For example I remember a coach telling me, "I know that kid is smoking. I am going to catch him and take his season away from him." I remembered being so disgusted with this way of thinking and wondering why this person became so hateful that he was focused on taking the child's one love - rather than helping the kid. Boone was not like that at all and supported me when I chastised the negative people.

Boone then asked if I would like to be an assistant coach and help him bring the 2002 varsity football team to that winning tradition we had had. I accepted his offer and was very happy to do so. The players were all fantastic people. Each and every one of them worked to be the best that they could. Some of these players were ironically on my first squirt team that I coached back in '91. I remembered the reason for giving the sacrifice and coaching for the love and respect of the game. It was awesome to be in their company again. These players had great heart and soul, and they were there for the same reason I was. They were totally committed, and their dedication showed by unconditionally giving one hundred percent. Every day I opened the weight room and all of the players were there waiting to take that next step into the discovery of how hard I could push their minds and their bodies. The physical gains they made were far more than what I had expected.

After lifting as hard as we could for the summer months, I had found that even the weakest players were now strong and confident. They started to train on their own without me now. All of the weight lifting and running was being done by the players which would turn out to be our team leaders. These elite players recognized what the team needed and did their best to guide the team in the right direction. I cannot say enough about these players and the assistance they gave the coaches. I didn't know what I was getting myself into when I accepted Boone's proposal to help him with this football team. In the lower levels of each sport lies a written rule of sportsmanship, great effort, and love of that game. The idea of having the development of players stalled due to poor coaching is a shame and a crime. To prevent this there has to be someone qualified and unbiased filling that coaching role.

I cannot say how important that teaching the lower levels of that sport, such as teaching the proper techniques, rules, and teamwork is. Those lessons help to build success in the future. A coach has to sell the idea, and then back the idea up with speeches and drills. These ideas are not about building a championship team, but about developing young players into responsible productive people. Those were the tools that were used when I was growing up. It was a combination of dedicated parents and coaches who mentored all of us into the people we are today. This team is a great example of how a group of coaches can guide a team of players and the players taking the guidance and use it for their growth. The lessons I taught and learned that season helped develop me into a better all-round person. From the time I started opening the weight room to the last time I stepped on the gridiron, I knew what the void was inside me.

The gift I was given from Boone that I am eternally grateful for has helped to develop me into a better coach and a better person. I hope that I can someday inspire kids like Boone has done. I know that I have tried to use all that I have learned in some sort of positive way. I try to be organized. I learned to watch the players and understand what they are feeling and thinking. I have learned some positive things from working in the prison as well. I learned to be assertive and have organizational techniques.

11

LIVING AGAIN

I knew what I needed to do to feel a little bit more like a compassionate human being. Even though I didn't coach football that next season, I was still in contact and talked to the players on occasion. I took up watching little league, soccer, hockey and other youth sports. I remembered what it was like to be young and playing for the love of the game. I remembered all the friends I had made through the years of playing these sports. I was watching these kids learning to play the sports they love. I didn't agree with some of the coaching and the biased favoritism that was going on. The great thing about being a non-parent coach is being unbiased. That appeals most to the parents and the players.

I think I became a better worker, as well as a better person, after being exposed to such positive influences. The prison no longer took as much energy from me, and my focus was clear. My new focus was to live and try to be happy. I stopped going to the bar, and cleaned up my love life. I knew that having positive people around me would help to keep the positive energy. I had to take things in steps. First I had to clean my personal life up. Second I had to stop wasting my idle time at the bar, and finally I had to do what makes me happy. After I did all these things I would still sometimes stop by the bar for a visit because those people would always be my friends.

WHERE IT STARTED

I was approached in the winter of 2004 by one of my supervisors at work about a hockey practice. Assistant Deputy Warden Jim asked me if I would come to the rink and watch a practice and give my opinion about his son Jimmy's practice. Later that night I drove over to the civic center and watched the practice. I gave Jim my thoughts on what was and should have been going on. I was watching a coach waste precious ice time by yelling at the players for not doing a drill correctly. I had decided to ask the coach if he needed some assistance on the ice to help these players understand what he was trying to teach them.

I approached the coach and asked him, "Hey, my name is Scott Kellett, and I coached back in the early 90's. If you need any help for on ice instruction, I would be more than happy to help you out." The coach became enraged and yelled at Jim, "How dare you bring someone to check on me! If you think you can do better you coach then!" I then politely stated, "I will." I felt that this poor coaching would affect the kids not only as athletes, but as young people as well. There is no place in life and sports for the constant negative yelling from a coach and the failure to follow up with some sort of positive.

I talked with Jim about what had happened and apologized for getting him into trouble. Jim said, "I am not worried about it. I just want the kids to learn as much as they can and have fun doing it." I totally agreed with Jim. I continued to talk to parents of players within the Polar Bear organization and found that some new blood and vision was needed. I was thinking about trying to become a coach the following season, but I was hesitant due to my confrontation with that coach. Jim was not content with me not being totally committed to coaching again. Jim would often bring up how special it is for kids to have a meaningful experience to help them to learn and love the game.

That following summer I was walking on my work assignment on the yard of the prison when I was approached by a co-worker, Frank. Frank was the President of the Polar Bear Hockey board and very influential amongst members. I remember Frank asking me, "Hey, we need a mite and termite coach." I was surprised because I thought Jim and Frank had talked about my confrontation. I asked what I had to do and when to do it. Frank gave me the details, and I gave my coaching request for the mites and termites that same day. After I had given my request to Frank, I felt instantly better about myself and what I was focused on.

The next day I called my friend Adam, who has a son that would be on this mite team. I asked Adam if he would like to help coach, because it has been a long time since I was on the ice and directed a practice. Adam accepted and was nervous due to not being able to skate as well as me. I knew I needed people that were dedicated to the kids and their development. I have known Adam since grade school and played football in high school together. Adam and I spent some time before season planning and going to our Level 1 and 2 USA Hockey coaching clinics. I was really nervous because I had never coached a learn to skate program and it was very important to get these kids to love this sport as much as me.

After getting my coaching certification, I was busy almost every day trying to convince parents I worked with and anyone I knew of my abilities. Trying to build the program at the lowest level is not only the correct thing to do, but the toughest. I was scared about how I would do in dealing with the kids, with not having kids of my own to use as a learning tool. I was counting on the parents to help me to grow as a coach and to help me to teach these kids about what the game was about. What I didn't expect, was the enormous support that I would receive from hockey and non-hockey people. Hockey is a very hard sport to sell to some parents because of the costs of travel and equipment. The fact is, everything costs money nowadays. Yet the development of a child physically and mentally does not have a price tag. I know some people cannot afford it, but they should consider trying to do it because there are a lot of people who will help with anything to get a kid on the ice.

Winter is the longest time of year up north; therefore, most people who live up here love some sort of winter sport. The same theory goes if you live in the south where it is warm, the outdoor sports like football and baseball produce better numbers of talented athletes. I believe we need to keep the kids involved during the long six or more months of winter. I tried to communicate this to the parents so they understood the importance of keeping the kids busy. I attribute much of the success in my life to keeping busy and concentrating solely on sports. I believe that if a person loses themself in a positive thing like sports, that person will have success in life as well. Like the football team of 02'. These young athletes were an inspiration to not only the young fans who watched them, but to me as well. Each of those players from that team was a success story in the making.

13

⊰⬥⊱

MY SOUL MATE

A little after being asked to start coaching hockey again, I was taking long rides on the bike to help me to focus and relax. Ironically enough I was on a bike ride that would change my life and give me some new focus. I was in Duluth, Minnesota on my bike and visited a young woman I had met a few years earlier. Her name was Sarah. We went for a ride on the bike and went to a bar to talk. We had a bunch of the same interests. We started to talk on the phone day after day for hours at a time. We had many things in common, most of which was the definite love for hockey in general. To be quite honest, she is more of a hockey fan than I could hope to be. I knew that she was the one and this was almost too good to be true. We did everything together and the things we had in common just seemed surreal. If it wasn't us enjoying sunsets out at the cottage, it was each of our fondness of photography. Sarah was an excellent photographer and her ability to take action photos was second to none.

Before hockey season started she moved in with me, and we began to make some long term plans. Most of the plans had to deal with hockey in one way or another. She was amazing and very tenacious when it came to the game or anything to do with hockey. The only difference we really had at first was that she was a New Jersey Devils fan and I was a diehard Red Wings fan. Our endless conversations about the NHL and college hockey would fuel our deep desire to be surrounded by hockey twenty-four hours a day seven days a week. We didn't always agree, and sometimes hockey was the reason behind some nasty arguments.

38

I thought that having so much in common was a direct reason for some couples to stay together through thick and thin. I knew from her great attitude towards the kids who would be playing the following winter that she was going to be a great help and support. I didn't realize at the time, but she would be the calm voice when I was angry or upset. Sarah helped with all paperwork and assisted me with everything I needed. The true fact is that she loves to be around the kids as much as I do. The upcoming hockey season is something I couldn't do without her.

MITES AND TERMITES

In October of 2005, we had hockey registration for the Polar Bear hockey organization that I was going to be coaching for. It was a great group of kids that showed up who seemed to be looking forward to playing for their new coach. The only thing about kids is that some get very nervous and scared of the new people that they were introduced to. I did the best I could to put on a smile because I was in fact just as nervous as the new players. As I paced nervously waiting for each future Polar Bear to walk through the door, I noticed many friendly faces. I got a little bit more relaxed with each young player I talked to. Many of the young players were talking to me as if they had known me for years, which made the new experience easier for all of us.

The gracious volunteers who helped to hand out equipment and register each player did an excellent job, and I was happy to be in such great company. I saw that each person was dedicated to the program and gave their time without hesitation. The hardest part about being a volunteer is that some people take for granted what each person is doing for their child. It always seems to me that the ones who are gracious are the ones who are always volunteering at any moment's whim. The night went great and we fitted many kids with their new hockey equipment. I got to see my potential team on paper and there were more kids than I expected on the roster.

The hardest part after that was waiting three weeks for the season to start. I was ready for the challenges that the season would bring. I was prepared for anything that would come my way. My first coaching experience was filled with ups and downs.

Along the way to coaching this mite team, I found that there was a new obstacle in the way of each team in the local area. The jobs here in the Upper Peninsula were far and few between. I could see many of the youth sports had suffered great losses because of the terrible economy in our area. The sacrifice would have to be greater and more than I had anticipated. A decision would have to be made between Sarah and myself about how much of the financial weight we were willing to take. Sarah is a fantastic lady, and she showed it by unconditionally supporting the decisions I would make for the improvement of hockey here in the Ironwood area. With our first practice only days away, there was much to prepare for myself.

I knew that total sacrifice and belief would be the only way that the players and parents would stick with the hockey program. The poor economy was an obstacle, but if I put my heart and soul into this I knew it could succeed. I felt the financial struggles for the area were going to last for years to come. The numbers of kids in any sport would not improve unless endless devotion was in place.

I wasn't sure what to do to get this thing started and what approaches to take. Not having any kids was such a disadvantage. I counted on my assistant coach Adam for this support and help with young children who I did not know and really didn't understand. I was prepared to understand and to learn about this new experience. I knew after dealing with prisoners on a daily basis that I needed to adjust my tact with the kids. Like all things in this world, learning new things can be hard but rewarding. My ideas for the players were a little advanced, but as some of the parents were telling me, these kids are like sponges when it comes to learning.

With my nerves out of the way, I needed to get some things in order to get this season underway. The first thing I wanted to do was to call all the parents and introduce myself over the phone. I gave the parents all the necessary information like, practice times, equipment, and asked that they get all their paperwork into the registrar. Every parent I called was awesome to deal with and helped me to gain more confidence. I started to feel for the very first time that I was doing the right thing. I didn't want to coach because of control or to say how great of a person I was. I was doing it because I knew I had great things to teach the kids on and off the ice. I thought that if I could make a difference in one of their lives all of this effort would be worth it.

My next preparation was to get all the termites notified of practice and answer all questions. The number of kids that had signed up for the learn to skate program was astounding. It was going to be difficult to keep up with all the kids on both sides of the ice. I wanted to be as organized as I could and make things as enjoyable for all the players as well. I would doodle with drills and times needed for each segment of my practice. I tried to give little breaks without wasting precious ice time. The first practice needed to be run so that it would get the kids interested and help them to love the game as much as I do. I tried to prepare for any obstacles that I might face and to adapt and overcome any unforeseen problems.

The last preparations I had to do were to get all my paperwork in order. I had my roster set with all the correct spellings. I had to double check all the birthdates and make sure they were in the correct age class. I then needed to get my stick re-taped which Sarah did for me. Not cool that she never has played the game but can tape a stick better than I can. Sarah and I went shopping earlier in the day for a medical kit that USA hockey requires that each coach should have available to them. I loaded up my pucks next to my hockey bag, and I double checked that all the equipment that I would use would be in the bag. The last thing I would put into my bag was all of my practice plans with my drills and my rosters.

One of the problems I had back then was that USA Hockey made it mandatory for every coach to have gone to coaching clinics. Frank (president of the hockey board) and his wife Kim had already planned on being at the first practice to give me any help and support I might need. The unsuspecting thing was that I had student coaches who were waiting to go on the ice. I was very appreciative of the assistance they gave. The student coaches were young players that had big smiles on their faces, and in return all the kids from ages 3-8 were in awe at the big kids that would be on the ice with them. These kids Cody, Josh, Andy, Jimmy, Josh, and Andy were standing by the doors to lead these kids on the ice for the first time. I was very thankful for the positive attitudes these kids had and how this was a great way to set the tone for the night.

The zamboni made its last pass and you could feel the nervous energy in the lobby of the Civic Center. The players knew it was almost that time to hit the ice and begin the season. As the zamboni exited the rink, the side doors closed with a loud unmistakable sound, and as the ping of the metal handle to open the door to the rink sounded, all of the kids looked back at me for the go ahead to head out on the ice. I gave a great big nervous smile and told them "Hit the ice!" I skated as a coach for the first time in more than a decade. The smell of the ice was like the spring thaw that touches your nostrils and makes you remember the past years of hockey. I did a couple of laps to loosen up my legs and blew the whistle to get all the kids at center ice. I still remember what I told all the players, student coaches and assistant coaches. "Everyone have fun and give one hundred percent." I then directed the termites to the west side of the rink and the mites to the east. I gave Adam a quick rundown on how we needed to work on skating for the days with some games along the way. I told him I needed to be on the termite's side since most of the players were lying on the ice from falling.

I went to the termite end and began to give loud instructions to the student coaches and some of the parents who were on the ice to assist. We brought out the pushers to help with the balance of the new skaters. Some of the advanced skaters liked doing their own thing, so I just rolled with the punches and let them have fun. I wanted all of the student coaches to stay with a group of kids, which was nearly impossible due to the forty plus kids on the termite side of the ice. The practice was an hour long and we were only ten minutes into it and my back was already hurting from bending over and picking players up off the ice. After the student coaches developed some sort of organization, I found a chance to go to the mite end and do some work with the new players.

I will never forget the smiles that those young kids gave me when I arrived at the mite end. Kyle who was eight years old and bigger than all the other kids was shy and didn't talk too much at first. Gabrielle was an eight year old girl that was very determined and never quit smiling for a second. Johnny Clemens, Adam's eight year old son, was a little small but had some very quick feet. These three players were the first that I had a chance to work with one on one. I saw some flaws in their skating at first and knew that as a whole we could work on drills to address these mistakes and correct them. I had a chance to observe every player on the mite end of the ice and had a plan for a second practice.

The hour and a half practice was quickly coming to an end and most of the termites were ready for bed, some kids were already off the ice and some were crabby from being exhausted. We helped the termites off the ice, thanked the parents for their patience and then went back to the mite end of the ice to get them ready for their send off. I told the kids that we had practice that Thursday from 4-5 pm and asked them to give me some ideas of some drills they would like to do. These kids helped me to believe that their young lives would forever be changed in some positive way. I believe that the work you put in to something will pay for itself in time. During this first practice I was happy and had some fulfillment. Adam and Jim were more than happy and saw the kids give their all. The last line of business was to somehow get time off of work for the games so I wouldn't miss any games.

I took my skates off that night and sat in the locker room by myself for a few minutes. I felt a great deal of pride and knew I was hooked. I was thankful to so many people for helping out and making this difficult first night a time to remember. I have not had many days like that, but I know I cherish each and every one of them. I knew that there had to be a ton of preparation done to make this perfect for the kids. I thought that if I were to get completely organized, I wouldn't make any dumb mistakes. I learned through work that using logs and making notes was the best way to keep organized. I went to the store and bought some paper and began to take notes. Although it was my first practice I wanted to be thorough and exact on my thoughts. I also needed to sell my ideas, not only to the players, but the parents as well.

The following Thursday the mites had practice alone. I had to have my first parents meeting and give my ideas and thoughts on the upcoming season. I prepared for the practice just like I did my first. I like to challenge the kids as much as possible and remember from when I coached before, that they would respond. I wanted to go a little off the grid for my drills. I wanted to do more advanced drills at the end of practice and try to mold each players skating. I was thinking about how to flow each drill until the advanced part of practice, and then at the end do a fun drill.

The idea I had was to complete a log for each and every kid for each practice and a separate one for games. Sometimes I would be too busy or forget some crucial information. Doing the best that I could for each of the kids was the only thing I needed to do. Those kids were giving their all, so I needed to do the same as well. My preparation was the key to being organized to a point of being almost over prepared. The logs I set up had each player's name and the date of practice. I would log how they did overall at practice and any flaws that they showed in their skating. I evaluated their performances on effort, ability, and if there were any other factors such as being sick, that affected them that night.

For the second practice, I tried to get their legs tired and then work on skating technique. I knew that the most important idea was to get great edges and dig them into the ice. Almost all of the kids had a dramatic and definite improvement. I gave a few water breaks throughout the practice and chatted with some of the kids during the break. I found that each of the players had their own special personalities. As for the players as a team, they all gave everything they had on every drill. Even though there were many flaws, each player and coach did their best to correct them.

Some of the kids from this team were very hard to understand. I think my not having children of my own affected me at the beginning because I was learning at being a coach and a parent at the same time. The disadvantage of this would be noted by the simple mistakes made. I didn't push the kids as hard at first due to thinking that they were a little weaker or wouldn't advance as quickly as I previously thought. It seemed everything I thought I knew on how hard to push the kids I was very wrong about. Adam would help me to adjust to the new idea that the players could take more advanced skating. I needed to go back to the drawing board and make a newer practice plan.

The players from this team are a special group I will never forget. It seemed already that I was a new person and I saw things differently. I thought more positively about things at work and in my personal life as well. It seems that I was loving life again and these kids were the cause. Each of the players had very different levels of skating and some were attributed to their love for the game. Some kids didn't love hockey as much as the other kids. Some parents seemed to ask themselves, "What I am doing here," because they never played. But for some, I was nothing more than a baby sitter. The sad thing is I never met some of the kid's parents. They didn't care or didn't want to go watch their practice or their games. And from talking to other coaches this is not just in hockey, but other sports as well. After seeing this poor parenting, and there were only a few, I felt sad on how a person couldn't take the greatest interest in their kid's life. It is something that puzzles me still to this day.

The third practice is something I will never forget and always be more cognizant. I was skating by the lobby area when a man got my undivided attention. I took a lap on the ice stretching out with the other players when it hit me. I knew I had seen that man before. I will not say his name only that he was a registered sex offender. I was enraged by this persons gall to come to my practice and be in the same area as these great kids. I immediately left the ice trying to act normal and asked the man to go in the breezeway for a quick chat. My adrenaline was pumping so hard and I had a ticked off look on my face, but I needed to be professional for the kid's sake. I asked him what he was doing here and he replied," I am here to see a buddies kid." I asked who the kid was and he couldn't come up with an answer. I told him, "Get out of here and don't let me see you here again, tell your buddies the same. If I see you here again you are going to jail." I said this without blinking staring into his soul.

I never saw him at the rink again.

I felt that working around scumbags gave me an advantage to see them before the common citizen would. It is something I still do to this day; I look around the lobby from time to time just to make sure. I didn't tell the parents for a few months but I felt what I did was right. Adam is a police officer and I confided in him about my actions. Adam said that being a coach and an adult was our responsibility to look out for these kids on the ice as well as off.

The players on this mite and termite team were a promising group of kids. I told them, "Have your dreams, there is nothing wrong with that." I told them and their parents that if they want to be an NHL player I believed it would happen for them. I loved the idea that each kid I coached would leave the rink with a smile on their face. I believed in these kids and felt that winning would not be our primary focus. For some people winning is the only thing. This makes it difficult to sell to the kids if they have this mentality. I would do my best to explain to the players, to always do your best and have fun.

The termites were filled with kids that had a blast each and every time they stepped on the ice. The players were fun and always made me smile. The student coaches did their best and had a little fun themselves. We didn't do much other than some small games and tried to keep the learn to skate program. Although some kids would not return, the ones who participated would excel. The termite group was a total success and some kids were moved up to the mite end due to their gains in skating.

As for the mite team they were a bunch of kids who all were very coachable. As I looked at getting some lines together due to the cup league games only a week away, I needed to look quickly at some of the kid's strengths and mold them into a position. I tried not to have a player stick to one position. I think the utility of being versatile on the ice is invaluable to any coach. These players needed captains to lead them on the ice and I had made my decisions on who would lead this team. I chose Kyle, Jonny, and Gabrielle. The players are all equal but captains are needed to ask the referees any questions.

Kyle was a more physically developed player and would have a great season. Kyle would do anything that I would ask and really loved playing the game. Jonny was a quick player with some nice skills. Jonny would give this team the voice the team needed. Gabrielle was always in a good mood. Her positive attitude and always support of her teammates was something I will always look for in a team leader. Alex, Andrew, Warner, Matthew, and Mitch rounded out the team with players who were all very coachable and were equally competitive.

Alex was the son of a friend of mine from high school, and he was very friendly at first but had his mother's temper. I knew that Alex loved hockey as much as his uncle and grandfather, did who I also knew from my younger playing days. Alex was a rare find, he was coachable. What that means is that he would not complain about anything ever. Alex did what was asked of him and he excelled because of this positive attitude.

Andrew was a really good kid and needed to be motivated from time to time. He has to be one of the luckiest players I have ever coached due to his scoring from time to time. Andrew worked well with his teammates and can take whatever criticism I gave him.

Matthew looked up to his older brother on the team and took a different role as he did dual duty as goalie as well as forward. Matthew was a happy go lucky kid and was always in a good mood.

Warner was a skilled forward and his skating ability was outstanding for his age. Warner was the impatient one. He got bored easy and needed to be challenged steadily.

Mitch was one of those players who played with his emotions. Mitch was a solid skater and would do anything that any coach asked of him. Mitch would help this team any way he could. Mitch would be a solid leader in the future.

In every practice the kids gave everything they had. They learned about some of the finer aspects of hockey and a little about life. Each player on this team would be effective in some way during the upcoming season. I thought I prepared the players for the challenges I set in front of them. Each player would respond in some way to make them better. I had prepared each player as I logged their positives and negatives when it came to skating. The parents got along really well, which really made my job as coach so much easier. The last step was to prepare for games.

I wanted to train the kids early in their hockey career the discipline of any sport. The ability to give everything on your shift, then get off the ice. Think on your feet which would help them better understand the game. With all of these challenges the bottom line was not about winning, it was building for a better future. I want the best for these kids and have them work in making it happen.

The next weeks brought a new era, the players had begun their season with a goal to have fun and play hard. All the teams in the cup league were placed by geographical location. Our opponents were Ontonagon, Iron River (WI), K-Bay (L'Anse and Baraga), Iron River (MI), Iron Mountain, and Negaunee. The problem with living in the Upper Peninsula is the distance between cities. The travel is a big negative, with the price of travel going up. The dedication begins with the parents. The commitment can be a financial burden, but is well worth what you get out of the experience.

The teams we played in northern Wisconsin were Ashland, Iron River (WI), Lakeland, North Lakeland, Park Falls, Eagle River and Rhinelander. These teams are around and hour and a half or less of travel. It is good to have teams closer and play them more often to help keep costs down. It seems living on the border of Wisconsin has its ups and its downs. Even though it takes six hours to get the mackinaw bridge we still feel that Michigan is our home. We are Yoopers, people living in the UP (Upper Peninsula of Michigan). It is like a pride thing. The kind of pride that draws you to dig deeper and try a little harder.

The season would start with the kids having great fun. The kids had a chance to meet other players from other teams and start to make some lifetime friends. It seemed like every team we played there was a bond to be had with one player or another. I really condoned that you play hard on the ice but have great sportsmanship off the ice. In almost every place we went the kids played hard and made new friends. I would do the same. Each team we played, I would try to talk to other coaches and parents. Most were friendly and were always up to talk hockey.

I found that meeting these friends would pay off for the players and myself. I wound up meeting coaches from other teams that I had played in the past. In North Lakeland the coaches were Jason and Scott who, I had played against from mites through bantams. We were always fierce opponents but now we were coaches trying the best for our teams. I think that this beginning would solidify some lifelong friendships that many young players would benefit from.

North Lakeland was our closest place to play and the kids got to know each other quite well. Buddy, Jacie, Caleb and Jacob would make up some of the team that I would get to know quite well. I liked how these players didn't take their feud off the ice. It is hard to get some kids to let their competition go when they get off the ice. The older they get the harder it gets. The teams would compete in tournaments as well as games. The reason I love going to North Lakeland is because it is an outside rink. It brings me back to my roots when I was young playing, when most of the rinks were outdoors.

Another outdoor rink was in Iron River, Wisconsin. Jeff was their coach and president of their organization. Jeff had two kids playing on the team Madelyn and Carter. Jeff is an excellent guy and his kids were always great to be around. The Iron River team was always in a good mood and we enjoyed playing them. This was another reason to stay coaching and to enjoy the total experience. Iron River was not only cool to be at because it was an outdoor rink but the fact they had 2 outdoor rinks made it special.

When we played Ontonagon I was pleased to find out that another old competitor was coaching their team. Jeff who I played hockey and football against had a son named Noah on the team. Jeff and I remained friends throughout the years. We went to college together and had many of the same interests. Ontonagon has a long reputation for being tough as nails and not easily beaten. This team would be just the same. The rink was not outdoors but it might as well have been since it is the coldest rink I have ever been to.

The termite's only action of the year was a termite jamboree in Iron River, Wisconsin. It was a very cold day but the kids played their hearts out and had fun. The hardest part of playing in the colder environments is to get the kids warm in between shifts. Iron River did an excellent job putting on a tournament. The warm up shack was big enough for all the players and always had hot cocoa for everyone. The biggest thing for the kids is the swag they would get at the end of the tournament. Every kid went nuts for those goodie bags.

That first season was a learning experience for all of us that participated in it. I thought to myself that these kids are much better than my old team was. I learned a great deal about coaching and kids that season. At the end of the season I evaluated what the kids have learned and if I did a good enough job. I am my own toughest critic. Like all learning, there were some flaws I needed to work on. I did like to coach the mites but I thought I would be better at coaching a level higher. I knew that I was going to attempt to be the squirt head coach the following season.

THE SECOND SEASON

The next summer brought a glimmer of hope that this season would be better than the last. Adam asked if I would help him coach little league. As always I accepted the offer to help Adam out. This would give me a chance to stay busy during the summer months. Even though little league doesn't have a coaches clinic you have to go to, the internet has an abundance of drills and skill progression that you can use. Adam did a very good job coaching the kids. I didn't do much other than support Adam any way that I could. I have played baseball since I was very young so the mechanics were easy to teach.

That summer taught me one big lesson; the kids are not all equal. Most of the kids I really enjoyed being around but there are some that are destined to be trouble. I found that some kids, if they don't have the discipline at home, they tend to be very resistant to any discipline. These kids I could see being the ones in trouble for the rest of their lives. I had a blast coaching baseball, the American pastime. It was good to see a new variety of kids. I tried politicking some parents to come and play hockey the following year.

At work, I think I was a pain to some due to I couldn't stop talking about hockey and how excited I was for winter. I was trying to recruit players steady. I knew that hockey would create better athletes in other sports. The balance, coordination, and the strength the players gain will transform into other sports. I found that the players could hit the ball as good if not better than the other players. In football the players were not hesitant to any physical contact. It seemed to me that they were faster than other kids. I have some strong beliefs because of the way I was brought up. The basis of these beliefs is by the blood, sweat, and tears that we shed trying to make this world a little better than we found it.

I did my best to try and support youth hockey. I tried to use my abilities to help these kids become great. Sarah and I tried to do anything to support these kids and to make some special memories along the way. These special memories are the beginning of their own trip. The pavement is being set for these kids and where they go from here no one knows. This second season is very important because their learning and development is at such a crucial time of their lives.

Preparing for this second season would be more fun and interesting for me. These kids would show their skills at a more elevated level. The challenges would be tougher and I would bring the game to them. The coaches really need to be a part of the growth more now than ever. Adam was going to coach the mites and I agreed to help him to develop those players as an assistant coach. I saw lots of potential and talent in the mites. Adam had a great plan and really gets a great effort from his players.

I could see the future was going to be very bright. The talent was unbelievable. The players were all coachable and had that drive that every coach hopes for. I remember talking to Brad with a shy son Tyler hiding behind him, about how bright the future was for these kids. Micki was the same deal. I talked to her about how special this group of players was and it seemed like all the parents who were interested were also very dedicated to their child's development. Together we all were paving a future which none of us would ever expect.

The kids returning wouldn't be enough and I would have to ask some parents about moving their kids up one level to play. The unfortunate thing about living in this rural area is the number of players from year to year is lacking. The team needed two more bodies to have a functional team. I asked two parents if we could move them up to the squirts and they agreed. Alex was one of these players I moved up with his strong will and motivation, I knew he would succeed. The returning players Andrew, Jonny, Kyle, and Gabrielle would also be moving up due to age.

The players that were on the existing team were very talented and were all awesome kids to coach. I was a little nervous because new faces bring new challenges. These kids that were already on the team like Justin, Beau, and Nick were the only ten year olds. We had a short bench and a group of talented players. Nick was our goalie and his skills were fine-tuned by his father Eric, who was helping me coach. Beau was a smaller player who played a lot bigger than he was; his skill level was far exceeding anyone on the team. Justin had the rawest talent. He was probably the fastest kid I have ever seen at that age.

The squirt age is a great age to coach and in my opinion the most important. The problem is where you start. I looked at my books and all the drills that were on the internet. I came up with a solution. You could go into systems and how to win hockey games or you could keep developing the players. I thought my strongest point as a coach is the development of the player. Systems are for people smarter than me; I want work on what I know. I have studied these players and I wanted to start a tradition. This tradition would be for each player to set goals and work on beating those goals. The players seem to respond to what challenges I threw toward them without complaint.

This squirt team would not fare as well in the victory column but they would make great gains in their skating ability. I felt that each and every player used the quality ice time to help themselves. The hardest thing as a coach is to try and break bad habits that players develop. The problems if not corrected could last the remainder of the players career. This could affect that players future plans in the sport. I didn't want my practices to back off my big plan. This team and these players needed to keep on track with their skating.

Hockey can sometimes be a ship in a storm. You can lose control if you don't take the little precautions. It can also be your comfort in tough times. As a player, if you trust your team and work hard, only good things will happen. These kids would feed off each other and work hard. I found that Justin and Beau as captains did an excellent job. When something needed to be done from one game to another, they didn't disappoint their team and helped the team to be the best that it could be.

Our team was invited to a squirt tournament in Iron River, Wisconsin. I had developed a great friendship with Jeff and it benefited everyone because of it. Like all the tournaments in Iron River it was fun for the kids and cold for the parents. The tournament was true to form, excellent games and the excitement of playing in the semi-finals against North Lakeland for the right of playing in the finals vs. Iron River who had won their bracket. I think the players hard work paid off in crunch time.

We began our semi-final game with North Lakeland. It was overcast and a few snowflakes here and there. The wind was howling and you could feel it burn your skin. The team was really pumped and took the ice without complaint of the cold. After a short warm up, Beau took center ice vs. Buddy. The game started at a very fast pace. Both teams were unfazed by the bitter cold that was hampering both teams. Justin was doing his best to carry the team just like he always did, but Beau was the hero of this game. Beau was one of those players who could not be stopped. Buddy, Beau, and Justin were all lighting the lamp. With one minute left Beau tied the game and sent it to overtime. After a short break we took the ice and Beau said to me," I got it." Beau didn't say much but he was a true leader and a good captain to this team. Not long into the overtime Beau sealed the game with a beautiful wrist shot.

The championship game was another Iron River classic game. Tough to the end and back and forth. Nick shined in net making many great stops, even though he was frozen, he didn't complain. The stinging toes and fingers didn't affect either team. The howling wind slowed down enough for the sun to shine a little. Carter was just as good in net for Iron River. The game was a back and forth battle with goals from Jonny, Justin, Kyle, and Beau helping us to cap off a great day and take the championship home.

The highlights of the season would define this team as a whole. Sometime in January we had the UP finals which are where the winner goes to the state championship round. Although we had not done well in terms of wins, Nick was spectacular in net and helped us to compete at an elevated level. Justin showed his speed and Beau was his gritty self. The other players did excellent. Gabrielle was tough on defense. Jonny was smooth and back checked hard. Andrew made some surprisingly nice plays. Kyle, who I tried to transform into a defenseman, was excellent, and Alex was tough and showed he will develop into a nice player.

The last highlight of the season would be our tournament in Appleton, Wisconsin. The team would go to this tournament to have fun. I wanted them to enjoy the pool and have a team movie. I didn't know what to expect from this tournament but our team seemed ready to play. Being that we had a short bench I asked a couple of mites to join us for the tournament. Caleb and Warner came to the final tournament. I felt that these kids came together for the short time they have been together. The things, I remember best of the weekend were two games in particular.

The first was the semifinal game. We played a team from Crystal Lake, Illinois. This team was very tough and we were tied with three seconds left. I called time out and had the kids sit down to relax. I drew up a play hoping to get a last second goal. The faceoff was designed to have three key players. Jonny was our best faceoff man, Beau was our most aggressive, and Justin had our fastest shot. The idea was to have a quick faceoff to Justin for the quick shot and Beau was to bring the garbage goal. In a split second, Jonny won the faceoff and Justin shelved it over the goalies shoulder with no time left. We won and were heading to the championship game.

The second game didn't disappoint. The kids faced a tough Appleton team and our confidence was high after playing an emotional game. It seemed like fate for the kids to improve each and every day. I think some of the players were starting to understand and believe that they were good hockey players. I think that their belief transformed their play to another level. This team right now could compete with anyone. In the second game it was a back and forth battle. At the end of the third period the game was tied. You could feel the tension in the building and we had quite a few chances and their goalie made some quality stops. Nick was on his game too, making many game saving stops.

The game was deadlocked in an overtime tie. As the tournament rules go the game was supposed to go to a three player shootout. The tournament director came to me and said that they bought more ice time to play another period. They resurfaced the ice and I remember talking to Eric stating that this game wouldn't last long as both teams were exhausted. The faceoff started the second overtime and within one minute the game was over. Appleton scored while Nick was screened. Although we lost the game the player's total season was a resounding success because every player got better. It made me proud that the coaches had helped to develop such good hockey players.

I looked back at the second season and I felt that I may have found my niche. I saw some really talented players develop before my eyes. I thought this special combination of good players and dedicated coaches was an all-round win-win situation. The next season would need to be different in some way. I was going to stay at the squirts to help keep the program strong and keep the players developing. I had an idea for the next season and some of the players moving up would be a big part of my plan. Being an assistant on the mites does help with the transition for the players and parents.

That next summer Sarah and I took the next step in our life. We got married and began a new life together. We couldn't figure what we could do for a honeymoon so the following week we went to a AAA tournament to see Warner Young play in Blaine Minnesota. We wanted to go watch some hockey and spend some time with the Young family. We were astounded at the size of the rink and thought how cool it would be to coach a team in a big tournament like this. We were not sure where the future would go but we were going to do it together.

16

OLD FRIENDS

Sarah and I didn't do too much after the season had ended. We tried to make every players games in other sports. Some of the events Sarah and I went to were little league games, soccer games, AAA hockey games, and Pop Warner football. I really enjoyed going to these games. I felt at peace and the players would make sure they said hi. I think to be a successful coach or mentor you have to care about the players all equally. It sometimes can be tough to be unbiased due to the underdog, who you want to do exceptionally well. You have to keep all the players equal. The team didn't need any undue distractions. I thought of how to keep with the fun practices and challenge the kids at the same time.

A coach who I highly respected and learned a lot in the past two seasons was Tom K. Tom was my friend and unfortunately he had a horrible coaching experience. I saw the worst nightmare that a coach could have. He had parents who were loyal to another coach and would treat him with the most disrespect that I have ever seen a person take. I felt awful for Tom. The guy devoted his time no kids on the team. Tom is a classy guy too, he didn't lash out at the parents that were treating him like he was garbage. He picked his head up and worked his practices to the best of his abilities. Tom is very knowledgeable and loves the game. His dedication is admired by me and I knew that having him help any team that I am coaching is a win.

Learning from Tom was a great new experience. I was not all correct on the skating development for the players. Tom and Jim would show me how to get the players on their edges. I was big on using the edges but some of my practices didn't flow as much as I would have liked. Tom was great with assisting me with this. Tom always had drills written up. Some he saw done by colleges and some he made up on his own. Tom has a kind and caring demeanor about him. His ability to communicate with the kids is just what is needed to help any team get a little better.

We had the making of something special here. You could feel it when you walked into a room of these players. That they were focused and having fun. I would add any coach, student coach, or volunteer that wanted to help in any way. I looked at the oncoming season as our first mite team back together. Friends reunited for a little hockey. I knew some of our second year players had more talent than were showing and somehow we, as coaches, needed to tap that. Last season set the tone of a group of kids that would progressively get better. I knew these kids as well as I knew myself. I studied them and I cared about all aspects of their young lives. With caring about your players I think the development goes smoother. The kids responded well to me, and I in return, would listen to their problems and be a mentor.

Bringing this team together with new players and coaches was something I welcomed with open arms. The players were all friends and they would do anything for each other. I had big expectations because the development of some of the players was so advanced that I would have to look for new ways to challenge them. The winter hockey season of 2007-08 was a reunion from the beginning to the end. The new squirts we had were a talented group. Caleb who was a speedster that I called crazy legs, it was mindboggling how quick he was. Ronnie was not a very good skater but his superior balance made him an outstanding goalie. Moving up to play for us was Warner. His freakish talent was scary. His sister was on the team and made it convenient for their parents for travel reasons. The players having their last season as a squirt were Kyle, Jonny, Andrew, and Gabrielle.

The decision I made early was to hit the edges hard. Skate those kids as hard as I have ever skated any team. They had the drive I just needed to keep the pedal to the medal and have our supporting cast keep us on track. I was focused on the squirt team alone. I wanted to keep focused and not take any attention away from our team. We had our leaders, and our developing leaders in Alex, Caleb, and Ronnie, to develop into a solid tough team. I knew they would never quit and I would never stop believing in where this team could go. The idea of playing team hockey was folding in with their skating, flowing drills into each other. The first practice would set the tone with our high paced drills and pushing each other to the next level.

Tom's greatest help to me came in work he did in the net with Ronnie. Tom and Ronnie became instant buddies and they worked really well together. This was the base of our team. Jim Young and I would try to mold the forwards to a cohesive unit. The defense was mine, I wanted them to be gritty, own their ice and be solid, two-way defensemen. I was thinking if we solidified a defensive game we could transition into a quick offense, since we had great team speed. Our defensemen were much disciplined and protected their defensive zone. It was a philosophy, but I wanted the players to think on their feet and see the ice. I thought if we gave enough small games to assist in their development that they would start to learn on their own.

We played all of our regular teams in the season again. We tried to mold some players into positions they didn't like, but they would all make sacrifices for the team to become two way players. I would use games as a learning tool to help develop aspects of their game. As for our players, I was proud of their efforts each and every day. Their efforts became ultra-aggressive. This would bring some arguments between some players and me. Jonny and I would argue from time to time. I really pushed him to be a leader when his team needed him most. Sometimes this resistance would cause a temporary hardship between us. Adam understood what I was doing. Our team was becoming so competitive that they would take losing a little hard. When players become so enthralled in the games it is easy to focus on of winning.

Gabrielle was becoming a little feisty and her crease was hers. She wouldn't back down from anyone. I was happy that she improved each and every day. Kyle was tough at defense, he was a quiet warrior. He did quite a bit of scoring from the point. Alex is disciplined and listened to everyone who tried to help him. Alex was developing into a good player and a solid leader. Caleb was feared because of his great speed and athletic ability. Andrew had improved, but needed more discipline. Ronnie had a great first full season and his future was looking bright.

We entered a few tournaments that winter and did really well. The players seemed to play at another level whenever it was tournament time. We won all the tournaments we were in but one. In our district play downs, we came up a little short, but I was very proud of how the kids played. I thought their development and skills were at a premium level. I was happy with the coaches and the efforts they gave. I was most happy that these kids were a team from day one. They looked out for each other on and off the ice. They respected the game and always played their hearts out. I think the biggest highlight of the season was that the team battled back from a 4-0 deficit in the championship game of the Stevens Point tournament and we came back and won 6-5. It was our signature as a team that we wouldn't quit.

17

CRAZY EIGHTS

The next summer Sarah and I did our usual. We went to all of our player's summer sports to cheer for our players. The focus was now on the upcoming 08-09 season. I knew that our team would have short numbers yet again. I had an idea of who we could move up, but in doing so we would have a very young and inexperienced team. We didn't know who was going to be coming out. This season had many positives. Some of our players that we had were great leaders and their skills were above average. I wasn't sure if we were going to ask 1 or 2 players to move up. I was hoping that we wouldn't have to move anyone up if we had enough at sign-ups.

I wanted to do something different before the upcoming season. I wanted to do dry land training with any players who wanted to get into the groove before the ice was put on. Most of the squirt team showed up and other age groups were well represented. I wanted to get the kids involved and have some fun. We had our first dry land in Wakefield high school's gym. It was perfect for all the things I wanted to work on. The stair workout along with the ability to do short sprints gave these players the ability to cut loose and give one hundred percent.

When sign ups came it was as I had figured. We didn't have enough players. I asked Adam, who was the mite coach again, if I could move up one or two players. Adam didn't really care, but now the convincing would have to come to some of the last year mite parents. I had asked Bob whose son Brett was one of the advanced last year mite players. Bob didn't want Brett to move up yet. I asked if Tyler could move up next. His father was more than happy to have Tyler move up, although he was concerned with his abilities. I explained to him that Tyler would be fine and I thought his skills would advance far beyond our expectations.

The last set of parents I would ask would be Micki and Craig. Their son was C.J. and he was a very big kid. Nothing came easy to CJ, but he had a work ethic that I admired. I hoped that moving CJ up wouldn't hurt his development. I knew from being an assistant with Adam on the mites, that these kids had their potential. CJ reminded me a little of myself. He was coachable and he never quit. Micki and Craig said yes to my request to move CJ up to the squirt team.

The players who work without complaint and believe in what they are being taught I feel they are destined to succeed. Jim already wanted Warner to stay at the squirt level due to his great play from a season ago. We had three eight year olds on the squirt team. Caleb and Alex would be our captains. Gavin and Mitch would be very solid players, moving up to the squirts. Ronnie would be our sole goaltender. The team had everything I could have hoped for. We had speed, skills, and toughness which would pay big dividends in this season.

Our coaching staff was comprised of Jim Y, Tom K, and myself. I believed our work would pay off down the road, but our main focus was on developing great players in the years to come. Every year I try not to put too much into winning, for fear that failure would hurt the player's development.

I tried to really push the edges again since it was showing in our player's development into awesome skaters. My personal goals were to find a way to be competitive using our skating and hustle. I wanted to show that our team had no weak spots. I think the kids confidence and self-worth is just as important as their skating. My log of each player needed to be more defined and work more towards the total player. I also wanted to really work on a power play and penalty kill through the use of small games. Lines needed to be set and worked out so that we could get the most out of the players who complement each other.

The lines I wanted to have was an all eight year old line. CJ, Tyler, and Warner would have enough talent and I thought they would gel together perfectly. As for the other line, Gavin and Caleb were a great compliment since they hung out together. Mitch and Alex would solidify the defense and I would count on them often to help Ronnie out. The idea of each player complimenting each other was a new concept to me. I had always put the weakest player with the strongest, due to balancing the team. I thought the new concept would challenge the players and make them even better.

The season had some excellent moments. Our team was not only the youngest squirt team in the Upper Peninsula, but we were one of the best teams. They came to every practice ready to do better than the last. I would try to match up players in practice to develop some competition. This competition amongst players would drive some to play better and create a little drive. If there was some anger between players because of the competition, I would try to quell it with some team building exercises.

The season had a bunch of highlights, and each player participated to the best of their ability. Every game was a battle and we were prepared. This was the first season that I had a team that would never be blown out of a game. At our play downs we played better than any other team played before. We were one of three teams to move on from the play downs to Houghton, Michigan to play in the district finals. It is astounding that we did this with such a young team. They proved that their hard work and their determination paid off. The team earned their spot at the districts, and even though we failed to move on to the state tournament, the Polar Bears represented and played great.

We played in a tournament in North Lakeland a few weeks after the play downs. Our team wasn't accustom to the outdoor rink and playing on harder ice. It was a great day because we made it to the championship game vs. Stevens Point. They were a bigger and faster team, but we had a determined younger team. Caleb carried us in the championship game scoring a hat trick. I am still unsure how the team did so well in the darkened rink. The lights were not as good as they were at the indoor rink, but the kids adapted and won the championship.

The last, but the most memorable thing that happened, was that Alex went into a corner and his stick went into the boards funny, breaking his wrist. Alex came off the ice and was crying. Alex was tough as nails and I have never seen him cry before. Alex said his wrist hurt and he couldn't move it very well. I called over his father to look further at him. I asked the referee if I could get a player off the ice and Alex then went to the locker room.

The current game was unimportant and I couldn't take my thoughts off Alex. Immediately after the game I headed straight for the hospital. When I got there Alex was in the E.R. getting x-rays. I remember walking into his room and seeing a cast on his lower arm. My heart dropped, not because of losing a player, but because I dread seeing any kid hurt. Alex was upset and understandably so. I tried to console him with some kind words of encouragement, but it didn't really help. I texted the team to let them know what happened to Alex. Right away team mates started to pour into the ER. Warner, Caleb and other team mates came to the ER to see Alex. No matter what I said his team mates brought his spirits up.

Alex was a tough kid and just missing one practice was tough on him. The team was so close that they were like family. Each player felt a responsibility to one another to try a little harder. Their drive was like that of none that I have coached before. My hopes as a coach were coming true. These players were developing at an alarming rate and getting noticed by other teams as well. I truley admired the drive they had. As for Alex, he would be the leader I thought he was. Alex had a cast on but could play with a foam piece over it. Having to wear a cast made Alex very unhappy.

It is hard to explain to a 10 year old that I am more concerned for his health than some game. During districts I found Alex trying to pull his cast off so he could play in districts. I was so angry with him that Sarah and I went to a local hardware store to get some foam to put over Alex's cast. We went back to the hotel and found Alex trying to cut off his cast. I was mad at first but then understood what it meant to Alex. He was one of our captains. A trusted leader of his team. His toughness and determination was admired from the whole team. We wrapped the cast and Alex could play. Thankfully Alex didn't injure himself but I will never forget his determination.

At the end of the season we had been invited to a tournament in Park Falls. I had met one of the coaches from the other team Tim, who had a couple of sons on the team, Seth and Aaron. It was a fun but emotional tournament. I had some parents ridicule some of my decisions and did it in front of the other team's parents. I didn't like to hear any criticism in front of other people. I wasn't sure what had happened, but some were not happy even though we had won and everyone played well.

After a hard week of practice I would have to deal with some more interference between the coaching staff and myself. Some parents think they can manipulate by intimidation. This first was the time in my career where a parent who was unhappy due to their player not improving. I didn't feel I needed to explain to a parent that our focus was on the team not on the individual. For the sake of trying to keep the peace, I tried to talk to the parent and they became belligerent, which caused me to walk away. I thought that the focus needed to stay on the team and I wasn't going to try to treat anyone special due to them being the squeaky wheel.

The season was all wrapped up and I received a call from Scott, from Park Falls late one night. He was calling to ask me if I were interested in coaching a AAA hockey team in Milwaukee Wisconsin. I was totally caught by surprise and was trying to figure out if this was a joke. After a pause, I accepted the head coaching job with Eric as the assistant for the 96' Tundra team. I then hung up the phone and told Sarah about what just happened. I was honored to have this great opportunity. I hadn't coached anything with checking before, but I was excited, because that was my cup of tea.

THE TUNDRA

I was so excited to coach a AAA hockey team that I started preparations immediately. I received the phone numbers of all the players and called them to do a practice. I didn't know any of these players location, on this team since they were older and from Northern Wisconsin. I wanted a central practice so I scheduled one in Lakeland, Wisconsin. I needed some help to evaluate our talent and figure out lines, so I asked my cousin Larry to come and video tape the practice. I wanted to be flawless in executing practice and in getting to know these players.

I had a chance to talk to Eric and we both agreed to let the players use their skills and not weigh them down with some different systems. I figured that these were not good hockey players, they were great hockey players and they had the skills to adapt to any situation. I didn't want to make any mistakes by over thinking either. Eric is one of the smartest people I have ever met. In the short time I have known Eric he has taught me more than I have learned by all my years of playing and coaching. This team was a blessing to myself and to any team I would coach from here on out.

Finally the day of the practice had come around. I was anxious about meeting the parents and I didn't have the stellar credentials that other coaches in AAA possess but, I pleasantly found out that each and every parent was awesome to talk to and every player was very personable. After a brief introduction to the parents, I went and talked to the players. Then we got on the ice. They wanted to play and they wanted to win. The first player I talked to was Brandon, he was a tall kid from Eagle River. You could tell he was a great leader by the way the other players respected him. I asked Brandon to be my voice to the players if they didn't understand me.

We hit the ice running and I tried to flow the practice as much as possible. The players didn't do any complaining. They were receptive to Eric and me. These were by far the best players I have been on the ice with, ever. Their skills were far superior to mine and they were giving their best effort. We had a two session practice with a break in-between. I wanted to observe all of their hockey skills and having the practice on tape only made it better. Larry and Sarah's opinions were very helpful. I found that I got the players names quickly and we felt like a team. I didn't know what to say because I was in awe by the great talent on this team. At the of the practice Eric and I felt really good about how the players responded.

I talked with other players who were chosen to play on other Tundra teams and felt that they had great talent as well. Warner, Jimmy, Tyler, Roman and Justin were among other players that were on the tundra teams. I wanted to do something special for my Captains this past season. Sarah and I chose to take Ronnie, Caleb, and Alex to Milwaukee with us for a fun hockey weekend and see the Tundra team play. I knew all three boys would be excited and we had some other plans to get them introduced to AAA hockey.

We were on our way to Milwaukee and all three boys were in the car ready for some hockey. I was wondering if I would have to out think another coach because these players were so awesome that I was confident that at the end of the weekend we would win the championship. The teams that were entered were two from St. Louis, one from Milwaukee, one from Chicago and one from Minnesota. It was a melting pot of talent. The players on this team were focused and I wanted all the players to show up in the morning before games to have a team stretch.

The night before I ran into Jeff in the lobby and asked if his sons were playing. The only one playing was his son Caleb. Caleb was a very nice player and a true talent. I asked Jeff where he was going to have the boys play hockey next season. Jeff said he wasn't sure but he wanted Caleb to get some training at defense. I offered if he came to ironwood I would give him all I had to help him to become a two way player. I figured it wouldn't hurt to throw an offer out. Jeff just smiled and we continued to have small talk discussing the boy's future and where this tundra experience would take us all. The lobby was a huge party of all the Tundra teams. It was all fun and games tonight but you could tell it was down to business when tomorrow come.

In the morning we met in a convention room and did our stretching and team run. I felt we were ready for whoever we were to play. I was hoping that this would be a beginning of a great experience with many more to follow. We arrived at the Petit Center, which in itself is an awesome sight. It is a speed skating rink with two hockey rinks in the middle. The rinks have to be reached by walking underneath the center where the locker rooms are located. I couldn't believe that this was even happening. The experience in itself had the boys even more pumped up than they previously were.

The teams we played were good, but they were no match for these Tundra players. We walked through with relative ease and reached the championship game on Sunday. Later Saturday night I went and watched the game of the two St. Louis teams. I talked to the head coach after the game and asked him that if he wanted, he could take the better of his two teams, and play us. I explained that I wasn't trying to be a wise guy, I just wanted the kids to get a challenge because I came down here for great hockey. The coach looked at me and agreed.

I told a few parents about what I had done later that night. Most of them laughed and thought they would never do that. I wasn't sure if he was going to, but I wanted to give these boys a challenge just like I do for my own regular season team. Sarah and I saved our surprise for Caleb, Ronnie, and Alex. We took them to the Milwaukee zoo. The boys had a great time as did Sarah and I. I felt that the boys deserved this trip because I do ask a lot of them to lead the team and become the light that helps lead them. I think they had fun swimming with the other players and all the running around they did at the hotel. It is a long hockey tradition that the kids will play knee hockey in the hall ways. I don't think other than being at the zoo I saw the boys for more than five minutes.

The next morning we did our normal routine. Stretching and a good breakfast. We then headed over to the rink for the championship game vs. St. Louis. I didn't see the other team come into the arena but when we walked up the stairs I was surprised to see that the opposing coach did change his team and mix the players. The only way we could tell this was done, was that they had different colors on their last names on their jerseys. I was speechless but I did approach him and we would have our hands full now. The game started out even. St. Louis scored soon after the game had started. There was a quiet air on the bench. After the first period we were down, I could now use what coaching skills I had.

I told the players, "You can choose to be better than them or you can lie down and get beat by a team that has half the skills that you do." I went on to explain, "Leave it all left on the ice. You can rest on the ride home with your head held high." They responded very well and had a very intense look about them, Zach wanted to play forward and I thought, "Sure maybe it is what we need." Zach scored right away, tying the game. Then Nic would light the lamp. Finally Sam would score and we would begin to pull away. We won the championship five to one. At the end of the pictures I talked to the players one last time and left the building. I grew attached to them all because they reminded me of our players back home.

I knew I was hooked and the experience is one that all coaches should have. The experience from start to finish was one of the greatest of my life. The parents were all positive and the players were all great to deal with. I was forever thankful to Tim and Kim for giving me the chance to coach this team and for Scott for, having the confidence that I would do a good job. I was hoping that this could be a bridge for the existing Polar Bears to get a chance to play summer hockey if they wanted. I think all of the players cherished the great experience we had in Milwaukee. Eric and I became lifelong friends and I still continue to learn from him and his great coaching.

When I got home from Milwaukee, I found that over half of my team had emailed me and wanted to do another tournament. I immediately looked online for a tournament that would be competitive and help the players to develop. I found a tournament in Duluth, Minnesota. I emailed my team and found that some were on other AAA teams and would not be able to play. I also got together the 2000 birth year for the same tournament but a different weekend. For this team I would try to fill in some of the vacant spots with my own players.

Eric would call about a week after Milwaukee and ask me if I were interested in helping him coach the 96' Blizzards. I didn't even hesitate. I accepted and was eager to take on this next challenge. The summer hockey with the Blizzards would consist of ten practices and five tournaments. The players were already chosen for this team and I found out that most of the Tundra players were either on this team or played on another. During the duration of the summer I found out that playing at an elite level is not only difficult, but each player has to be dedicated beyond anything that I have coached before.

Playing other teams from Green Bay, Stevens Point, and Wausau showed me just how small the hockey world can be. I loved to see other players from other teams who I got to know from either talking after a game or seeing them at the hotel. The players all had one thing in common, they loved to play summer hockey. It seemed that the summer hockey family resembled that of our winter club. The only difference is that the summer team is not from the same area.

The one thing I can say for sure is that coaching the Blizzards helped to keep my interest in coaching summer hockey. I found that some of the people from the Tundra and the Blizzards made it hard to co-exist and they had to be separate from each other. Being a part of summer hockey is exciting and it gives you an interest in having more competitive hockey in your life. The only way I can explain it is that when you take a ride at an amusement park and it was so fun that you can't wait for the fair to come back so you can ride it again. That's the feeling I get when summer hockey comes around.

I am sure that this great experience would give a little boost to the players who would make their AAA teams in the future. These players who were developing would make big gains by playing with players that were equal to, or better talent than they were. In return they would bring that edge to their winter club teams. I also believed that this confidence, that the players received from their AAA experience that I would also make the same gains as well. It was awe striking to see so many of my players playing in an advanced skill level and competing. I was always honest if a player was ready or not to play at this level. Some parents didn't agree with my thinking, but that was alright since I would not discourage them.

That summer I saw so much talent throughout the AAA season. I saw that Minnesota was stacked with talent as I had previously thought. I also found that our talent was as good if not better than most in those hockey hot beds like Minnesota and Chicago. I knew we were on the right path. The path to help these young players develop and give them a chance to help them achieve their dreams. It seemed that every path I saw developing was only the tip of the iceberg for these young players. In the future they would be asked for other AAA teams as well as the ones I would organize. I found out that some players would respond differently to positive and negative reinforcement.

I knew that as a coach of a AAA team that some players had to hold their weight. If they were not performing or didn't prepare themselves for the game, they might need to be sat down on the bench. To me this was a new concept. I wanted them to respect me, but also play their heart out. Benching is not always a tool that helps the player. It is a necessity when that player doesn't correct their problems with the way I feel their playing. I have never benched anyone for not giving a one hundred percent. The only times I have done this is when I felt the player was tired and could not play to the expectations of the coach, or they have given up on trying. This thinking is a learning tool. Only a few players would get enough drive to make up for their mistakes by giving a little more effort and earn their right to get back on the ice.

The Lake Superior Stars tournament would happen in August. The first team I would take would be the 96' team with some new faces. I found out the hard way on how a team that is so talented and well coached can decimate even the best of players. The loss came to the fault of the coach, me. I found that my own cockiness and over confidence would underestimate this great team. The team we faced was Canadian and they were big and fast. There was nothing we could do as a team. For the first time coaching AAA I was speechless to the incredible talent we faced. We got beat in every aspect of the game. The players didn't quit, and we played our hearts out the rest of the weekend. I now knew what it took to be truly elite, and what I was giving wasn't enough. I needed to be more of a stickler on the little things and make quicker decisions.

The weekend ended on a good note and I expressed how proud I was of the players for not quitting. I vowed that the next week I would be totally prepared and I would not make the same mistakes twice. I thanked the parents and the players for coming to play for us and I hoped to get another chance in the future to coach them. I left the parking lot with handshakes and hugs. I felt so bad that I had let the players down. I knew I had to set the boundaries for the players. I knew this weekend was a very competitive elite tournament.

After a week of long preparation, I found that my confidence had restored to its normal self. I had thought out lines and how each player could help this team to win. I didn't want anyone to feel as I did the week before. I chose to take Brett and CJ to this tournament, knowing that their talent wasn't as good as some of the others, but that they could help this team win. I had also brought a few coaches to the bench, as I tried to get some coaching constant to my own, since Eric couldn't join me. I asked Tim, Jim and Tom K. to join me on the bench. I wasn't sure what the weekend would hold for us, but I was ready.

We played on a Friday night, not certain of what to expect. We played a local team from Minnesota right away. The kids came out playing hard and winning every battle they had. We beat the team big time and won eleven to one. I didn't want the kids to get over confident so I played it off that they were not as good as I had thought, but to keep up the good work and good things will happen. I knew we played a talented team, and I would wait to let the players know when to let up. I expressed to the team that they needed to keep prepared to play. I wanted them to get a lot of rest because we had two big games, including another Canadian team on Saturday.

On Saturday we played a team out of Thunder Bay, Canada. They were all fast and very skilled players. Their warm ups were flawless. I wasn't sure what to think because this was the same organization that beat our 96' team. Our Tundra team came out flying, the kids passing and making big plays to give us a lead to start the game. The rest of the game would follow suit. We won seven to one. The players left it all on the ice and didn't let off the gas. They were a very solid team but they couldn't beat us on that day.

Later that afternoon we played another team from Minnesota. They were not as talented as Thunder Bay, but they were disciplined in their play. Our players did not show any sign of fatigue they were winning all the races to the puck. Their efforts didn't come without a payoff. They had played themselves into a great place to play for a chance to play in the championship game, winning seven to three. We had to play the Lake Superior Stars who were hosting the tournament. They had not lost a game either and they were just as talented as we were. I knew it would be a great game, but I had no idea how good it would be.

The team arrived at MARS Arena in Duluth about an hour early so we could get some dry land training in and do some mental preparations for the semi-finals. I was preparing the team for one of the most important AAA games I had ever been a part of. We had to go into their rink, in their state, and win for a chance to play for the championship. The game started out on a fantastic note. We were leading in the first period half way through the second. Then they made a big push and came back to tie the game. In the third we jumped out and it looked like we were going to win the game. Towards the end of the third period the Stars made some great plays and tied the game again.

We were going into overtime tied at five and the team looked tired. I wasn't sure if I could motivate them, but I felt some players needed a rest, so I shortened the bench since their rules were 4 0n 4 hockey. Both teams were tired, but we had a group of kids who refused to give up. I shortened the bench and we began to play. With every shift the speed of the game picked up the pace. The players seemed to have found a second wind and they were determined to win the game. After each shift the players rehydrated and kept on giving their best efforts. The first overtime had come to an end deadlocked five to five.

The second overtime would have much of the same, this time it would be 3 on 3 hockey. Both teams going back and forth with each team's goalies putting on a clinic. I had seen many games but this was becoming better than any other game I have ever seen. The highlights of the game seemed to be our ability to come close and hit a few pipes, thereafter a large sigh from the crowd. I couldn't believe my eyes that these kids were machines. They had played two full periods deadlocked at five.

The Third overtime I started to become a little worried. These players were in great physical shape, but there was no way to prepare for this kind of physical strain on those young bodies. I now would use a full bench. The rested players would give the other players a chance to recuperate. I wasn't sure if we could pull it off, but I knew they were just as tired as we were. I didn't know how much they players could take, I just wanted the game to be over. The player's safety was in my mind, so between the second and third overtime I asked the players if they could go on. I didn't want the kid's effort to be for nothing, but I let them know this would be the last period. No matter what I wasn't going to put those kids in jeopardy. I told them that I was proud of them, but give it one last push, quick shifts and keep hydrating.

The third overtime would be the end of a classic game. Both teams came out flying, but refusing to take any extended effort to give up any unnecessary scoring chances. We were on the attack early and after many scoring chances, Lake Superior had a break away on our goalie. The goalie had been outstanding thus far and the Stars player made a quick shot and missed the net. Bobby fed the puck up to Seth. Seth skated past their defensemen and buried the puck past the Stars goalie putting this marathon to an end. I do not know what was said on the bench or what the players said all I know is the parents were crying with joy. Final score Tundra six and Lake Superior Stars five.

This unbelievable victory came with 6 periods being played. Two full games were played and we now faced a championship game versus another team from Minnesota. The team was the Minnesota Blades, arguably one of the best AAA teams in the state, maybe the country. I had an exhausted team who I felt wasn't going to go down without a fight. I was confident and you could feel they were too. The cards were stacked against us.

I asked the tournament director about who we were playing next. I knew the players needed to hydrate and get some good food to replenish what was lost. We were playing in three and a half hours. I was more worried about the fatigue factor and if the parents had listened to my instructions for the players to rest and refuel. The next line of business was to get my things in order and begin to prepare for the championship game. There was some tweaking to some lines and some defensive pairs I wanted to change up. I needed to think more defensively to let the kids gain back some energy.

The plan was to save any and all energy we could before the game would start. I wanted all the coaches to be complimentary and bring some positive energy. We went out on the ice and the Blades followed. I knew that our team speed and skill would not be better than theirs, since from front to back their team was solid. I called the players to the bench and sat them all down and gave a little speech to them about," our legs are ready, they are the ones who are nervous." The players responded with confident smiles. There was no more to be said. Towards the end of the 5 minute warm up I told the players do a couple of hot laps and return to the bench.

The players looked ready. They had the killer instinct and their eyes showed it. I set up our lines and reaffirmed how proud we all were and this game, win or lose, they were already winners. We gathered for a breakdown and went to the faceoff circle. The arena was quiet. A quiet that puts a chill down your spine. It started to feel like destiny and these players were not going to give any second effort.

About the second shift in there was a freakish play in our zone. A player from the Blades flipped the puck in front of our net and another Blades player smacked the puck in for a 1-0 lead. It wasn't anyone's fault, just a good hockey play. The rest of the period was an incredible pace but dead even in skill. We ended the first period just like we started, flying to the pucks and winning most of the battles. This did nothing but improve our teams confidence.

After a short break between periods the players looked alive and ready to play. We had a good, loud breakdown and went to the faceoff circle. Warner told me that his line would own this period. Tyler and CJ were on Warner's line and they were playing awesome the whole weekend. The other lines were playing fantastic too. Brett Heil was even playing far beyond my expectations. I was proud of my Polar Bears. Caleb was solid and made some terrific plays in the second period. About half way through the second period Tyler buried a shot by the Blades goalie. The deeper the game got the more our Tundra team gained confidence.

The end of the second period came and we were winning most of the races to the puck, but the game was tied 1-1. Our team confidence was growing and the crowd was getting louder. We went into the locker room filled with smiles and they didn't seem to be tired at all. The coaches and I stood in the hallway and let the players bask in their accomplishments. It may not seem like much but when you have played a ton of minutes more than another team, and to still be competitive with an elite team is a lot. I went into the locker room and gave the players what they needed. I said," Today is your day, not theirs. Take what is yours. Win the championship. You have worked hard and showed everyone here today that you are not good players, you are great players. Go on that ice and take what is yours!" The players ran out of the locker room with a great amount of energy.

We took the ice and the players skated some hard laps with an excitement that only champions possess. The team gathered around the goalie for one last war cry. They huddled around the goalie and gave some triumphant yells which could be heard throughout the rink. I was starting to get those butterflies but I still wouldn't look past this talented Blades team. The game restarted with the Blades coming out flying. Our defense played outstanding and cleared the puck quickly just as they were instructed. Our forwards back checked with quickness and with a purpose. Our fatigue started to show half way through the period. We made some mistakes, but our goalie was keeping us in it again. We had our offensive chances also but we couldn't capitalize. With two minutes left one of our defensemen fell down and I immediately called him off the ice because I thought he banged his head off the ice. As I called him off the ice a Blades player picked the puck off and ran it into our zone scoring on a great shot.

Now the players were tired and heartbroken. We needed a faceoff in their zone so we could pull off our own little miracle. As the game started to get to the end, our desperation grew greater. I told our players on the bench we needed that faceoff. The energy was off the charts. The players and fans were all standing in a nervous excitement. The time on the clock was ticking faster and faster. With 18 seconds left we had a faceoff in our zone and I called a time out. The players with long looks on their faces all sat down and looked at me. I found it inside of me to smile and give them the confidence boost they needed. I said," This game is not over! You have played nine periods today let's make it ten periods. Pick your heads up, We are going to win this game." The team was rejuvenated and ready to give one last push. I had Warner face off to CJ and ring it around the rink since CJ had the hardest shots. I then told all the players on the ice move towards the net and bang it in. We also had pulled our goalie to give us an extra attacker.

The faceoff was dropped and warner won it to CJ. CJ shot it around the boards in our zone to Tyler. Tyler raced it up the ice and passed it to Warner in front of the net. Warner took the shot and hit the post. The puck went into the corner and Tyler put the puck in front of the net as time expired. We had failed to win the game, but we played a great hockey team to a 2-1 loss. The players earned all the respect that I could give them. The day had been one of the greatest days of hockey in my life. The players who were obviously disappointed held their heads high knowing they gave everything they had.

We took a quick team picture then headed to the locker room. I was not sure of what I was going to say. I walked in the locker room and had all the players stop getting undressed. I remember saying to them," Today was your day, you set out to win a championship and you did something more. Each of you contributed in some of the best hockey I have ever seen. All of you are great hockey players and we will be back. Each team now knows the Tundra is not a push over. You have gave every team up here a reason to fear you for years to come. We are all proud of you and leave here with your heads held high." I then shook everyone's hand and left for the parking lot where I would address the parents. I thanked the Gerhke's for allowing me to coach and I thanked the parents for their dedication.

Sarah and I then left the parking lot after giving some hugs and more handshakes. We had a quiet ride home just thinking back about what a great weekend of hockey it was. I was already thinking of how we could improve and do some great tournaments next summer.

A PLEASANT SURPRISE

In the fall of 2008 about a month before we started practice I decided to do some dry land training. I invited everyone on my email who was affiliated with hockey. I got an interesting surprise. Caleb and Jacob were coming to dry land and Caleb was going to be a Polar Bear. I was totally excited because he was a great talent from Mercer, Wisconsin. Jeff wanted Caleb to learn how to be a 2-way player and a better defensemen. Jacob was going to play in Park falls the following year, but his dedication to hockey was evident. All of the squirts were showing up and had a hungry look in their eyes.

The focus on the season had begun already. I was training the kids for quicker feet and more leg explosion. I wanted to keep steady on the dry land because I have seen many of the summer AAA teams that do a dry land routine before each and every game. I was unsure of what the season would hold because these athletes on this team were in shape and had skills that I haven't seen before at this level. The focus of the team was to grow through teamwork and hard individual work. This team was different. There wasn't just one player to focus on there was the whole team that needed some kind of defensive attention.

It was only October and I was losing sleep already with the potential of this team. Kerry and Brian were dead set on having their son Ethan moved up to the squirts. Ethan was a young, very talented player, who was only 8 years old. I agreed to move Ethan up if the mite coach was willing. The mite coach agreed to the move and understood that Ethan was more than talented enough to make the move. Ethan coming to the team did a few things for the squirts. It gave us depth and another player that could play forward and defense.

The combination of Caleb and Ethan would begin to mold a good team into a great one. I always do lines and jot down other intangibles that the players have. The weapons on offense and the toughness of our defense would shape the squirt program into something we were all proud of. I needed to keep all of our two way players focused on their development and not stats. The concentration of talent was not towards any one player or line. The team already had a good vibe since they were all good friends already.

We had dry land training each Saturday right up until our first ice practice. The last Friday in October was our first ice practice. The first practice went smooth and each player seemed to compete against each other in every drill. This gave me a great idea. I would mold most of my practices around the competition with each other. I would spread it out with other players so we didn't have any grudges or hard feelings. The idea was to have the players compete against each other, and then I would have the two players be team mates in the small games we would set up. This worked fantastic and really helped to mold our team.

YOUNGEST TEAM

The team was only a few days away from starting our season with our first game. Iron River was our first game and they were one of the tough teams that we would be facing. We started the season with fourteen players, three ten year olds, ten nine year olds, and one eight year old. This would make us the youngest team in the Upper Peninsula. Our age did not show on the ice. We were a very skilled team that would compete with any team that we faced. It is funny, in all the worrying I do as a coach, our age was never one of them. I knew that this team, no matter how old or young we were, we needed to keep on the line and stay with the plan to keep concentrating on our edges.

The practices would be designed to work on all aspects of the game. I would focus on our weak parts of our game and initiate some sort of breakout play. I remember being in practice and wasting a ton of time breaking the puck out of the zone. The theory I had was to initiate the kids into visioning the play and how the options would unfold using their individual skill. I thought of this not only because we had talented players, but they were very smart as well. Another part of the puzzle was to have the mentors around the players. I wanted Jimmy, Jonny, Justin and Andy at these practices whenever possible.

The truth is, I felt that having mentors who wanted to help with the players development was a win win situation. I was trying to think of anything to help develop these players. Tom was returning to help out. Brian and Jim would also be helping coach. I wanted to help develop their minds as well. I wanted to keep a steady flow of conversation with the players and make sure that every player was talked to. I thought if they were to keep positive thoughts and great confidence it would carry on to their play as well.

I asked Jim if he thought we were on the right path and if there was anything we could do as coaches. Jim replied," I think we are on the right path, you cannot go wrong with concentrating on their skating." Jim and I had a bunch of conversations about situations and trying to help the kids advance with their hockey skills. I was entrenched with logging every single piece of information of each and every player. I had three log books. I had One for practice, one for games, and one for skating skills.

The first log book was for practice. I would log every drill in each practice and jot notes about how the team did in those drills as a whole. The second log book was for games. I would try to summarize the game as a whole and how each player did. The third would be how the team used their skills in each game. I would then keep tabs with the players' names and itemize what they did right and wrong. I would then look over the three log books and figure out what drills to do at the next practice.

I found out that some kids cannot be pushed as much as others. The pressure that some kids instill on themselves is sometimes too much. I had a few players sit on the bench during drills for a variety of reasons. There were some players who had bad cramps in their legs and some even threw up. I had some players get headaches. This to me was a sign of two things. One, we had an exhaust problem or, two a hydration problem. The problems took place during the first month or so. After fixing the problems and taking a few more water breaks the team was ready to move forward.

The flow is very important and using the logs to see where I could plug in different drills was helpful. Jim would often remind me to keep on track. The team was very blessed that we had very dedicated coaches that would help on and off the ice. Bob Heil and I became good friends because we were both dedicated and wanted to develop these kids. Bob said to me at one of our first practices, "If we don't make it to the UP's districts I will be very disappointed." I knew we were talented, but I didn't know just how we would stand up to the outstanding talent in the Western Upper Peninsula.

After the first week of practice using the logs, the improved skating was obvious. It seemed that the players bought into our philosophy and they were benefitting from it. Each player complimented the other. The competition was always fierce and the players would often get mad at each other from time to time. I knew from years of coaching players who had played for me in the past, that each player at this age has a very competitive spirit. The competition needed to be contoured to bring that competitive nature out.

Some players were a little timid at first but somehow we, the coaches needed to figure out what would help them to become more aggressive. This could be debated, whether or not a player can be taught to be aggressive or they could be guided towards a more aggressive nature. I feel that if you give positive encouragement towards winning small battles, the player will learn to be more aggressive to win those battles. I did this by having many two on ones and three on ones. This technique had great results. A player who is more skilled is put at a disadvantage with three other players against them. The disadvantage helps that player to think before the play unfolds. The team with the advantage betters themselves by perfecting their skills to win the game.

I found that using the combinations of players who don't normally hang out together is the best way to get team chemistry. It was evident of how to challenge the players and develop some type of ice animosity. I knew that if I could get two players who had great skating skill to challenge each other enough they would create an internal competition. The players did not all succeed from this method. Some players were too overwhelmed by the immense challenge, that they would not give their best effort. It took me many nights and discussions with coaches in and out of hockey to figure out a way to cure this. I would need the parent's assistance.

Some parents were fantastic to deal with and more than happy to help with anything I would ask of them. However a few parents were more than ready to not give any support. To make a student athlete you need a few positive things. You need the following One, a great family. Two, great friends. Three, great team mates. Four, great teachers and coaches. Without this it is an uphill battle. The difficulty even though you have great communication, is that some people want what they want. Even though the team's needs are everyone's concern, some people still think that an individual who isn't improving is one person's fault.

After our first weekend of games I found that we needed some player leadership. Our lines were not clicking like they should and something was missing. I made Warner captain because he was our most vocal player. Even though he was nine he was a good team mate and motivator. I would try to keep Tyler and Warner together at all costs. They had a perfect complement and Tyler could bury the puck. The other lines were in flux. I wasn't sure how to make that great practice team become a great game day team.

I had Nathan, CJ, and Mitch on defense. I wasn't sure about lines, I just tried to get some sort of compliment together on the ice. Nathan was not playing up to his potential. I wondered where to put him to give him the best chance to succeed. I will never forget Nathan looking at me with teary eyes saying, "I am trying but they are too fast." I was happy that Nathan was so honest and he was trying, but the speed of squirts is a big change over mites. I changed Brett and Nathan's positions which was my best decision all season long. Both players thrived at their new positions. Mitch and CJ were solid at defense and Brett did an excellent job with guidance from his father.

Now we needed to focus on our offensive scheme and how to help those players succeed. The offense would be molded by our two centers, Warner and Caleb. Each center had Tyler and Nathan on their wings. The combination of the nine year olds on each line was perfect. It seemed that if Warner had a bad game then Tyler would pick up the slack Caleb and Nathan were the exact same way. The forwards were quickly set as they molded well in practice and their efforts were easily noticed in the first games of the year.

Tom was working every chance he could with Matthew on every possible technique of goaltending that he knew. Whenever there was a chance, Tom was there sitting next to Matthew coaching him, and becoming great friends while doing so. I saw from time to time that Tom would bring in some sort of article or book on Hockey to show Matthew. Each coach was very different but we all molded somehow. The student coaches and their assistants were right along with the coaches as well. Each player had enough individual coaching to help them with any skill they needed. The mold was just how I wanted it, a harmony of good parents, good coaching, and great players.

21

BAD DECISIONS

The truth of the matter is that in the 2009-10 season, even though we had a ton of talent, some great parents, and a solid base of support from coaches it sometime wasn't enough. We had started every practice like the last, doing our base drills to perfect our edges and our leg strength. I think that the players would be happy doing anything on the ice, but some parents are never satisfied. The problem with sports today is every parent believes that their kid is destined for greatness, which is good. The bad is when they believe they know better because of outside influences.

People's opinions are a great thing. That is why I have so many coaches and student coaches on the ice. The parent who forgets about the team and focuses on their kid being the star or needs to be in the spotlight takes away from the big picture. The team has to be the focus and needs to be addressed. I found that this season would be one of my best as a coach, and most fun, was actually my hardest as a coach. Being that I work in a prison and shake off criticism and other negativity, I found it difficult to keep focused due to parent interference.

Our season started out like any other with dry land training before our ice was ready. I found that there were more and more kids interested in dry land training. It was a little surprising that players as young as 5 years old were participating. Kyle and Nick were both termite age but did their best to keep up with the older kids. I really liked the determination we had from the players year to year. I did my best to set up ladder drills and other quick feet drills as well. I tried to get as much done as soon as possible. No matter what I threw at the players they responded and didn't complain. It was this type of dedication that I think makes champions.

The ice was ready on the Saturday before our first practice of the season and I sent an email to see if the players were interested in doing some power skating. I was very surprised that there were a bunch of kids who wanted to skate and get their legs ready for the first week of practice. I needed to make a power skating schedule with lots of edges. With all the players who attended we had enough to buy two hours of ice. I started to do some new drills so I could make the practices more challenging. I would implement them right away since the players responded well.

The practices went great and my logs were right on. The players were making adjustments like they should. Their growth as a whole was very pleasing. I knew that the little bit of negativity needed to be squashed quickly, so I did what came natural. I confronted it head on. I called a team meeting and addressed the problems that were brought to me and the ones that were said behind my back. I wasn't mad or hostile at first. We had a meeting in a little locker room with coaches and parents while the players were on the ice with the other coaches. I had my first taste of the complex differences in parental thinking. I had some parents that wanted a minimum amount of games and on the other extreme, I had some parents that wanted as many as they could get.

This would be the beginning of a bad situation. The coaches figured that a compromise between thinking would be fair. We set our number of games in the middle. I figured this would not only keep the parents happy but the board as well. The argument over the ice time would only be the beginning. The negative feelings would only get worse as the season progressed. I have always had an open door policy with parents, players and coaches so they could talk to me or my assistants about any problem they may have. I was shocked that some parents thought so lowly of other players. I felt very disappointed about these feelings.

I found it hard to believe that some parents were so quick to be negative and degrading towards a 10 year old player, then I snapped and said, "I am tired of some parents putting down other players and enough is enough. This is how great teams fail. Each person who is unhappy goes somewhere else and plays or keeps your mouth shut. This team is going forward like it had in the past." The negative barrage was not only verbal complaints but emails as well. We were only in our season a week and there was already division in our team.

On October 28 we had our first practice. The players were surprisingly in shape and gave one hundred percent on each and every drill that we did. This by far was the best first practice for any team that I had coached. The players were energized and smiling through the whole practice. The feeling I had was indescribable. I felt such pride that these players were focused so early and they wanted to win. Each player had something to bring to the team. This team had every tool that it needed to be very successful. The coaches were just as dedicated. Each player had every coach compliment them and reassure their confidence.

Our first game was against Iron River, Michigan. They were an awesome group of skaters. I felt that this team would be one of the top teams in the Upper Peninsula. Starting at home was a great way to get the season underway. We lost the first game 7-3 and Iron River looked sharp. Our mistakes were capitalized on and now I had something to coach about. Iron River had a fast team, but we were just as fast and talented. Iron River had everything we had, good players, goalie, and coaches. We started the second game not intending on winning, but having fun. The players were ready and had a serious look on their faces.

We took the ice for the second game and something seemed different. There was more chatter amongst the players, Tyler and Caleb were joking on the bench before we started. I felt that the first game butterflies just got us off to a bad start. Matthew looked focused and was unusually quiet. Tom had spent quite a bit of time with Matthew and built his confidence back up. Caleb, Tyler, and Warner would come out firing and we ended up with a 3-2 victory. Mitch, CJ, and Brett had great games. Nathan Garnell was switched from defense to wing. The switch helped Nathan to gain his confidence and be more involved with the offense. The first year squirts were caught off guard by the difference in speed, but they made adjustments. The season had now begun and it was feeling like this team could compete with anyone.

It is obvious that all players are not as skilled as others, but everyone has a need for a team. Every player who has ever played for me has helped the team in one way or another. This team needed to have solid leadership from the players and I wanted to push others to better themselves to become that leader. This method I was using was all wrong. Mitch is a great kid and a great player, but I didn't give him captain because I felt it would make him angry and push him into a leadership role. I figured Mitch would be ticked off and do it to prove me wrong, but I was wrong, Mitch was so disappointed that he was more angry than improving. I didn't notice until his mom Vicki came up to me and told me how disappointed he was. I was devastated. I had made a very bad choice and needed to correct it.

Mitch was made assistant captain and he became the leader the team that I knew he could be. He even surprised me by using skills he had been working on at open skating. I was very happy that negativity wasn't a problem with the players, just the parents. The feeling I had as a coach was not a good one. I felt like for the first time in my career there was a division between parents. I was unsure and I knew that everyone didn't get along, but the big picture shouldn't be distorted. It was a bad situation and without support from some of the parents this negativity would come to fruition sooner or later. I just didn't know how bad it could be.

The team was doing a lot of practicing the next few weeks. Deer season is always a big thing in the Upper Peninsula so I made some of our practices optional during that time. I would not deny any player to go hunting and spend some special time with their parents. Only a few players missed and we kept on the practice schedule. On November 18 Jeff had brought stickers for all the players' helmets. Each player was overjoyed with this new present. I can still see the smiles from the players when they received these stickers. The newly decorated helmets with the polar bear logo looked really good and it was one of our moments that our team was becoming closer.

22

THE SLIDE

Our next game wasn't until November 28. Some players would be missing because of the holiday weekend. One of our parents came up to me and stated, "I want my son at practice on Friday. I told his mother if he isn't at practice then he will not be allowed to play." I then replied," I will not take away from family time. And I don't get involved with family problems. I coach and that is where it ends. Sorry but I will not punish a player for missing practice due to family obligations." The parent was furious because he didn't get to manipulate his ex-wife.

While in Iron Mountain on November 28, I found that the player didn't show and there was a rift between his parents. I vowed not to be involved and keep things professional. I told each of my coaches what was going on and they all agreed that we stayed out of family issues. I had not even thought of what the repercussions would be. The games were absolutely fantastic. The players did a really good job and every aspect of team hockey was executed flawlessly. We won both games 9-1 and 9-4 this game showed that every player on the team could have an impact. Warner scored 4 goals in the first and none in the second. Caleb didn't score in the first game had 5 in the second game. Tyler was a little off for some reason and his shots were a little high, but they had some smoke on them. CJ and Mitch both scored from the blue line. This balance is exactly what we had been practicing for.

When I got home I was pleased with the effort all the players gave. I began to log each player's positives and negatives. I found if I didn't do this right away that, I would forget crucial information. I did my logging and figured out what we could do for each player to improve their skills and their overall game. I wasn't home a half hour and then the season took an ugly detour. I started receiving emails about individual players basically saying two thirds of the team is worthless. I couldn't believe that a parent could act like this. It would be the beginning of an ugly part of the game. I was told in a variety of emails, things so horrible that I couldn't comprehend the hatred.

Some parents were unaware of the emails that I had received, but I wanted every person to know that I didn't care about their negative opinions. I am not a person where the squeaky wheel gets the grease. I have no problem dealing with conflict and I felt that somehow this would cure the problem. I didn't like whispering in the background or the cancer that can kill the best of teams. I talked with the coaches and we agreed that this was the correct path to deal with our teams problems. From here on out everything would change. The team was sliding into a tailspin that some wouldn't come out of.

I tried not to let the negative e-mails interfere with my focus. The negative comments, dirty looks and constant back stabbing began to eat at me. We were only two weeks in and I was already looking forward for the summer AAA season so I didn't have to deal with some parents. Sad as it may sound, I found it harder and harder to lace up the skates and do the thing I love. I had made many bad decisions that I was trying to correct for the good of the team. I didn't want some of the parents or coaches to see the constant attack I was under or to see what negative comments that were made about their child. The distorted view that becomes a cancer and eats at the purest of hearts needed to be dealt with.

I thought, if I had just told the parent off and went about my way that it would be all right. I was very wrong. About a month I noticed some other parents becoming angry about all sorts of issues. First there were the complaints about playing time. Playing time is a hard call that can easily be missed. But with the complaint, the coaches needed to address it and correct it. I had made sure that Jim and Bob who were running the door were not aware there had been complaints and to try and make it even as possible. Neither coach noticed anything out of the ordinary, but we did our best to correct the ice time.

The last and the biggest problem were the negative attitudes the parents was brought to our practice. I was noticing that some players refused to talk to other players. Seeing players ignoring other team mates was tearing our team apart. The problem was becoming a cancer on the ice. This was something I would not stand for and dealt with as soon as possible. The division in our team was obvious and I was going to start to bench kids for not being team mates. I thought instead of trying to make them play together and be really vocal towards one another, to make them pass and get along. The practice plan was being diverted by trying to do more team building exercises instead of our skating and small games.

We weren't even in the first month of hockey and what was supposed to be our best season was starting out like my worst. Jim had been really positive even though I was struggling to bring myself around the negative drama. Bob was very supportive also. He would make me laugh on the ice telling jokes as we skated around. This helped me to get back on track and keep the kids focused as well. I wasn't going to put up with any more distractions to the team.

The focus again was on the players and I really studied my logs closer. I could see the needs of each player and comprised a workout that would help improve everyone as a whole. We were only three weeks in and there were at least three months left so I needed to figure out how to keep the team together and still have fun. I wanted to do some unorthodox drills that were fun. The drills would all contour around skating and passing. I would then let each player pick a drill at the end of practice. I felt that this would give each player some feeling that this was their team too. The players really loved the idea of picking drills and had fun doing it.

Our team focus would not change. The season was about learning and fun, not winning. The players seemed to have as much fun practicing as they did in games. I would move on, and chose to ignore the negative parents. The next month of hockey would be a combination of great hockey and working on the finer points. I looked at December as a new start. Hoping that our team would not be affected by the negativity which was obvious by the obnoxious yelling by some parents.

I thought to switch practices again. I figured that our edges were pretty good and we would do some refreshers every practice. The change would be to help our players develop quicker feet. The change would define some of our advanced players and help our lower skilled players catch up faster. Mitch would always be challenged by the changing of drills, but he wouldn't quit and, always supported his teammates. The effort given by Tyler was steadily improving his game. Travis was improving and I was conscious to give him added support at every turn.

Our next games were against Park Falls. They were a highly skilled team and were coached by Sturgeon and Gehrke. Their teams had great systems and some really nice players. We split our games but our team showed a lot of heart by never giving up. The good thing is Travis scored his first assist and Brett had become our solid defenseman with CJ. The lessons learned this weekend were priceless. This is where Tyler and Warner's back checking would take control of a game. Caleb strained his groin and was bothering him all weekend.

The idea I had for practice the following week were to keep things fun with a ton of small games. I was pleased that we played an experienced squirt team and played so tough. The players were learning to use their skills in game settings just like we practiced. I was hoping that there would not be any distractions due to play downs coming next month. The next thing I wanted to teach the players was to do some moves that USA hockey would like their players to know. There are ways to use your stick to fool a defender to give yourself an advantage for a scoring opportunities.

Our next team we faced was North Lakeland. It was the first time that Caleb would face his old team and he was surprisingly excited to play them. I found that there was no bad feeling and the players all got along great. We played a great, clean game and the players from each team were more than ready to play again. We won the first game 6-2 and it gave Travis a chance to be in net. We won the second game 4-3 in a close, well-played game. Ethan was on defense with Brett and they were molding well together. Our second set of defense, Mitch and CJ, were equally playing good defensive hockey.

It was halfway through December and there wasn't too much negativity. The team had been playing great. We had another challenge the following weekend with K-Bay coming to Ironwood and Iron Mountain on Sunday. I thought that our Friday practice wore us down for the weekend games so I had to hold back and do most of our work on our Wednesday practice. This took away from having two solid workouts, but for the good of the players it needed to be done. I changed our practices on Friday to a light edge work out with more skill work, like passing and shooting.

December 19 would be our next game VS K-Bay. They were a team with three or four very skilled ten year olds. The team had some of the hardest shooters that we would face all year. They were like our team, in that most of their players could be two way players and help their team however the team would need them. We lost both games by one goal, but again we were very solid against good competition. Sarah and I got the kids a Christmas present like we do every year. We had found a good deal on jerseys and we bought one for each player on the team. The jerseys were two colors, which I would use in practice to assist with separating teams for small games.

On Sunday we played Iron Mountain again. We won the first game 5-3 and tied 3-3. The games were fast paced. Iron Mountain adjusted well to our passing, causing many turnovers. Iron Mountain scored on two shorthanded goals to even up the second game. I had been changing lines as well as getting some of our defensemen some forward time. I think that sometimes the players can become intimidated and not give their own skills enough credit. CJ sometimes was hesitant to pinch the near half boards. Ethan was fast and an excellent backward skater. Mitch was our fastest backward skater and sometimes went too fast for the pace of the play. These were good things to find out because it gave me a chance to fix some small problems with their individual game.

Tyler had been working on his shot and it was obvious because he was lighting the lamp on a regular basis. Caleb and Warner were our centers and they were winning most of their face-offs. Nathan and Travis were doing well at learning the wing position scoring more and more. Matthew was solid overall in net and was becoming a very solid goalie. It seemed like every aspect of our game was starting to come together. It seemed that the negative attitudes had subsided and we could get on with our season. I felt a little better, but I knew deep inside, that it was only a matter of time before there was something to trigger the cancer again.

Our team was winning a majority of our games and they did this without any pressure from the coaching staff. I knew these players were so competitive it didn't matter if it was practice or a game, all they wanted to do was win. I would give a speech before each game and reiterate that winning isn't the point of doing what we do as a team. I told them that winning is fun, but it will be more fun when it matters. It would matter when they are in high school, college, juniors, or the pros. The emphasis is strictly on developing the players and the team. I made sure that the players knew every game that we, the coaches were not mad about the mistakes they made, but that we would help them to correct those mistakes.

Even in two months of hockey the players would often talk about winning the state championship and how cool it would be to have their name in the rafters. I knew what their goals were I had given them some questions and I wanted answers. Most of the answers were about playing some sport after high school and others were about winning. It was surprising that most players wanted to improve as players. I now knew they had been listening and I was obligated to do our best to help these players achieve their goals. I know it seems like some big dreams, but those dreams are where reality begins.

The rest of the season held many surprises. The next games were at home and we were tuning up for the play downs in Ontonagon. On Saturday January 2 we played Ontonagon for the first time this season. They were talented and had a ton of speed. We were much younger but just as hungry. Teams that I have coached haven't beat them many times. Their organization has been consistent with solid players who can control a game. We took the ice at home thinking we were going to give them a tough game. We lost 10-2 the first game and I think our players were intimidated by some really hard shots.

Before the second game I told the players to relax and keep their shifts short. We had better legs overall and I told the players that. Some of our leaders really came out in the locker room giving each player support and being verbally excited. In the first period we scored the first two goals of the game. Matthew stopped 3 breakaways but Ontonagon scored two to tie it up before the first was over. I again started to juggle lines and to try to find some cohesiveness. The idea failed and we wound up losing, but our team didn't quit giving them a run for their money. Ethan on defense was going to be our permanent second line defenseman with Brett. It was evident that Mitch and CJ were very complimentary to each other. Our forward lines needed some tweaking, but some of our pairs were excellent together.

Tyler, Caleb, Warner and Nathan all had done an excellent job with their back checking. Their hustle would help this team win many games. Each player had been improving and the small games were working to further their hockey skills. Travis had been working as hard as he could and the coaches had been giving him some one on one time to further assist with his skating. Ethan, Brett, Mitch and CJ were gaining defensive skills far beyond where they should be at. I played defense my whole life and it was imperative that we work on solid defensive skills to be effective in the play downs.

On Sunday January 3 we played an "A" team from Ashland. Ashland had always been a good passing team and this team was exactly the same way. Our team came out fired up and showed it on the ice. The first period was all us. The kids were passing like they did in practice and we looked the best that we did all season. This is what makes a coach happy, not the winning and the losing, but the level of play a team works for. I saw now that the team had made a huge stride and was gaining total confidence in their teammates. I wasn't going to juggle lines any more I was certain that this was the best team on the ice. We won the game 4-1 and it was a solid game from every aspect of our team.

The second game would change many things for me as a coach. We came out flat and not ready to play. I forget sometimes that these players are just little kids and needed to be treated as such. I had seen the best we played all year, to the worst. I was dumbfounded and I tried every tactic to motivate them. Nothing was working this game. Our passing disappeared and players were arguing on the bench. We were down 7-1 to a team that didn't have the talent that we did. I was angry at first, but then I called a time out and called the players to the bench for a little chat. I always asked the players how they were feeling. I always tried to settle them down. First catch their breaths then go back at it. Instead, this time I told them," I don't care if we win or lose, just have fun. Pass the puck and next week we go to Park Falls for a tournament." The players as a whole were in better spirits and proved it by scoring 2 goals in a row. Caleb Baxter started the scoring by shelving one on a penalty shot. The game ended 7-4. Even though we lost we found that we could let each other down.

After the game we shake hands with all the players and coaches, and then pick up the water bottles off the bench. I usually then talk to the coaches before going in and giving one last talk to the players before they leave. As I approached the locker room I heard crying from inside. I was wondering, "What now". I walked in the locker room and all the players were crying. I was infuriated and yelled," What are you crying about? We lost, no big deal. It is only a game. Why are you crying?" Then Warner stood up and said with tears rolling down his face," He called us a bunch of losers." I knew who it was and I looked at Jim and Bob as they had fire in their eyes. They walked out of the locker room to talk with the parent who had belittled them. I told the players it was no big deal and losing is part of life. I tried to get their mind off the sickening display of parenting. I reminded the players that this was going to be a fun week of practice and it was a new year.

I walked out of the locker room and Jim pulled me aside and told me he had taken care of talking to the negative parent. Bob and I were still infuriated at what had happened and I was hoping that there wouldn't be an altercation with any parent's because of it. Jonny, who was in the locker room, came up to me and stated," What was that about?" I told Jonny with a smile," It's a loser who is trying to live through his kid." I still was in shock and Sarah was hostile over it also. It seemed that everything that could go wrong this season was going wrong. I just wanted to go home and watch some football. It was still bothering me after I got home because the phone calls were coming in steady and so were the emails.

At this point I just wanted the season to be over. I wasn't sure of what psychological damage had been done but I knew there would be issues for the rest of the season. I received a few more emails from our parent. I wasn't sure if he thought he could bully me to get his way or if he thought he owned the team. He wanted things his way and the emails were indicative of that. The basic message of the emails was that all the players stink except for his kid. He thought some players shouldn't even be on the ice. It had every negative thing to say about every player except his kid and a few of his friends. I didn't know how to approach this other than quit talking to him. I wasn't sure if he could be banned or kept away for some reason. He wouldn't listen nor would he conform to our team rules.

Bob was going to take this in his hands, even though I didn't pass the emails on, in fear that there would be some sort of physical altercation. I knew working in the prison system for all these years, that emotions run high when it deals with your kids, and the risk of an altercation is high.

I chose to keep the emails to myself and I refused to deal with the parent any further this season. I chose to ignore the ignorance and the delusions of grandeur that he had about his ideas. This season was by far my worst and I wasn't having fun anymore. I wasn't sure if I could keep a fake smile on and just finish the season.

I tried to refocus and become the coach that these kids needed. Only with the support of the coaches was a I able to get my mojo back. I made up my mind that this was going to be a great remaining season and I wouldn't let anyone or anything interfere. I got back on track by having a fun practice. The tournament the following weekend was just a bump in the road. I didn't want to go to the tournament, but the players were looking forward to it. I had been chatting with Scott all week about the teams there and how each other's season was going. I was looking forward to playing some different teams and seeing other players as well.

During the week I started to think about AAA and how nice it will be dealing with different parents. The difference is staggering in the attitudes you get as a summer coach, compared to a winter one. It is not that one is better than the other, it is just a nice change. It is nice that players can play at an elite level and still be productive. For some people who don't like AAA hockey or chose not to try out, they all need to understand that this is a choice. Some players play baseball, soccer, and football. Some like to go camping or do some type of travel. But for Sarah and I, we choose to participate in AAA hockey.

The following week was fun practices for the players. We did a lot of passing and shooting. I thought to change the mood I would back off some of the competitive small games and do more individual games. I found that if a mood change needs to happen the best thing to do is keep the smiles coming. On Wednesday night practice we were practicing accuracy shooting. It was very evident who was doing extra shooting outside practice. Ethan, for being eight years old, was really surprising. He was very accurate and had some heat on it. CJ had the hardest shot by far and Tyler, Warner and Caleb were talking their usual smack to each other. This friendly competition was exactly what we needed. I did have one bad surprise. Travis wanted to play goalie and he was disappointed that he didn't get a chance to play as much. I was going to put him in the net more, but I felt that he was going to turn out to be a great skater.

To help players choose where they would best benefit the team is a hard choice. Most of the players I coach are utility players. Utility players can play more than one position. The effort some give on the ice is indicative of their displeasure of the position. The goal is to make everyone happy. Sometimes it cannot be done, but to not try is doing the game, and the player, a great injustice. I believe that every coach should utilize their ice time as much as possible. Time constraints are a common thing for all teams, but the key is to make the time as useful as possible. I try not to build up any undue tension for a tournament. We, the coaches always try to keep focused on having fun and staying with our original plan of skill development.

Bob and I had a candid conversation about the things to come. We discussed how it seemed that when we make strides with the team there is always something in the way. The cancer that can overtake a team is astounding. I needed to have more parental support and I scheduled a team meeting for Wednesday. The parents needed to help me keep this team together and the obvious division within the team would not be tolerated. I needed to get the players away from the bad attitudes because some players were picking up on their parent's negativity.

We had a nice schedule for the following weekend. We played Medford and Calumet on Saturday. The stands were full and the energy was incredible. Neither our players nor our coaches knew what to expect out of the weekend. I just knew that these players had worked hard to become the team we all wanted them to be. We played Medford in the first game. We scored nine seconds in, which set the tone for the rest of the game. The game was fast paced and we looked like we did against Ashland with our great team play. We wound up winning the game 7-1. Tyler had 4 points along with a hat trick.

The second game we played on that Saturday was against Calumet. Calumet is from the Copper Country. It is a name given to the area of the northern Upper Peninsula for the Copper mines that they were famous for years ago. The Copper Country area is also known for its great hockey heritage. I always take any copper country team with the most respect. Every team I coach I remind them that if we play a Copper Country team, that we are in for a battle since they are all skilled and never give up. This team would be no different. I changed things again I moved Caleb to left wing so he could utilize his shot more like Tyler was on the other line. It was a great game with not much scoring until the third period. We scored 5 goals in the third and won 7-2. Tyler was busy again with 4 more points. It was now on to Sunday where we were in the semifinals against Park Falls.

Sunday January 10 we were playing Scott's team. They were fluent in systems and had some nice players. I didn't say much before the game. It was business as usual. CJ got the music going and the players were getting their equipment on. Jim and I were discussing having the players learn a new skill for this game. I wanted them to learn how to shot block. We had worked on it in practice a little, but now was a perfect time for them to show how they could benefit from their self-sacrifice. We went into the locker room and gave the players an assignment. Park Falls had great shooters and we could benefit from blocking those shots. I explained how to do it from our drills on Friday nights practice. The players were all smiling, agreeing that this might work.

We took the ice with the confidence of beating Park Falls and not looking to the championship game. The game went exactly like we wanted. They would block shots and get scoring opportunities because of them. The players were getting how to pass around their shot blocking. They were using the skills they were taught. The players had built a lead by blocking shots and great passing. We wound up winning the game 6-2 against a very good team. The players had earned their way into the championship game against the Wausau War Jacks.

It had been a good weekend for the polar bears. We had grown to understand what we needed to accomplish to achieve short term goals. The War Jacks were a tough "A" team that we had never played before. There were a few AAA players on the team but we had ours as well. This would not be an easy game for either team. The stands were full and the hallway to the rink was filled with players from Park Falls giving the kids high fives as they entered the rink. Our warm up had our usual drills to help the players loosen their legs and their minds. We lined up for the opening faceoff and the players had an unusually quiet tone about them.

The game started out rather slow and we were losing in the first period 2-1. I asked the players to keep with the game plan to pressure the puck and to block shots. Tyler and Caleb were pulling double teams which meant that our centers would have more ice to move around. Warner took advantage of Tyler being covered by tying the game in the first shift of the second period. The game would have great defensive plays by both teams and both goalies were outstanding. Warner deflected Mitch's shot to make it 3-2 in our favor. Wausau was a very tenacious team. They had pressured us as much as any team we faced all season long. The start of the third period was nail biting. The War Jacks had a break away to start the third period, but Matthew stoned them. The period went back and forth with no scoring. With 45 seconds left the war jacks called a time out. I knew they were setting up one of their best shooters and I had Tyler cover him. I wanted to set up an opportunity for us to score as well. We needed to win the faceoff and be aggressive to score on an empty net. Warner won the faceoff to CJ who passed it to Nathan. Nathan dumped it in Wausau's end attempting to kill off the rest of the game. One of the War Jacks made a bad pass because of Tyler's fore-check right on to Warner's stick. He buried the puck and we won the game and the tournament. Warner got the MVP, but our team was all MVP caliber this weekend.

After we received our trophy and took some pictures, Coach Scott came up to me and wanted to talk in private. He asked me," What is wrong with your parents?" I replied, "Not sure what you mean." Sturgeon went on to tell me," You win the championship and your parents still aren't happy. They were saying you don't know what you are doing and you are a terrible coach." I explained the problems that I had been having with some parents. Sturgeon understood because he was having some of the same problems. I told Bob and Jim about the comments and was trying to decide if it was worth bringing up. We only had one practice before the play downs in Ontonagon.

23

MAKING DUE

With only one practice the team needed to work on special teams and some good positive thinking about the weekend in front of us. I wanted to pound the 3 on 2's and do some 3 on 3 small games. We were also going to have a parents meeting and they were going to hear it. I had decided to give them both barrels because I was tired of the whispering about what was going on and we couldn't succeed with this negativity. I even had one player who refused to talk to me. He got his parents attitude and it wasn't going to change. I felt that all the time that Sarah and I devote to all the local youth sports, that it was an atrocity to be treated this way. I told the parents that I have had enough of the back stabbing. It was stopping here and I would invoke the 24 hour rule if it continued. Their poison is spreading to this team and the coaches were not standing for it. I also explained if players were detrimental that they would sit as well. There was no one person on this team nor would there be. I left the room after talking to the parents and told them if you had a problem Bob would take care of it.

The practice went smooth and I wasn't going to slow down. We picked up the competition and pushed the players hard. The players were ready for the play downs and so were the coaches. Tom spent more time with Matthew building his confidence and working on his core skills. This ritual was really helping Matthew to develop into a nice goalie. I then had a pep talk with the players at the end of practice that I will never forget. I talked to them like young adults. I said," You are growing up. We are all proud of you, parents and coaches, but we need to take it up a notch. We are a good team and all of you are good players. If you want to win you have to take it from the other teams because they want it as much as you do. Win or lose it doesn't matter, we are all winners." I then told Tyler to break them down and I would see them on Friday in Ontonagon. I asked Tom what he thought and he didn't have much to say other than enjoy the moment. I would cherish that advice.

Friday January 15 we played Iron River for our first game of the play down weekend. The game was its usual, close right to the end. We tied 4-4 and our nine year olds kept carrying us. Caleb, Tyler and Warner all scored goals. The evenness of our teams was staggering. We were much younger than they were, but our talent was equal. On Saturday we had two games. We were playing Houghton in our first game, another Copper Country team. Houghton beat out a couple of other teams to make it to the play downs. Houghton had some really nice skaters and I knew it would be a tough game. Our defensive game would prove to help us win. The thing I most remember was that this was Travis Collins first goal as a squirt. We won the game 7-1. Again it was a total team effort. The players did everything right and Matthew was tough in net. Saturday evening we played Calumet who had earned the right to the play downs from their own organization.

Saturday night's game with played Calumet would be one of my favorite games as a coach. Calumet had a tough goalie and some really fast skaters. This was one of the first teams all year that I believed was more skilled than we were. The game started out fast with nice playmaking from both teams. Calumet struck first, scoring a goal half way through the first period. Calumet ended the first with a nice goal that got by Matthew. We started the second period after a short ice resurface, with a steady barrage of offense. I remember feeling bad for Tyler as he hit 3 pipes in a row. You could feel the sway of the game in our direction. Caleb Baxter buried a shot and we finally got on the board. The game stayed 1-2 going into the third period. It was one of those periods where time went slow and my heart was pounding because of it. It was a back and forth game and neither side was scoring. With one minute left Ethan took the puck from behind our net and skated the puck out of our zone. I was yelling for Ethan to pass the puck because all five Calumet skaters were after him. But Ethan didn't pass it, instead he skated and made a move around a defenseman and scored over the goalie's blocker to tie the game. The game ended that way tied 2-2.

We had two games left to play and it was against Ontonagon and K-Bay who had beat us all year long. The team had done fantastic up to this point and I was feeling good about our chances to make it to the districts in Manistique. It was our only game on Sunday and three of the five teams were going on to the districts from the play downs. We played Ontonagon Sunday morning and we got beat bad 0-9. It was the same thing that happened two weeks earlier, our entire team failed to play. We were defeated by our lack of effort and I was at a loss for why. Our last game of the day was against K-Bay. K-Bay was a tough team with great skill and speed. The game would be defined right off the faceoff. K-Bay scored three goals in the first period. We needed to stay focused because there was a chance that we would not make it to the districts if we didn't play well. The second period was almost the same as the first, but we only gave up one goal. It was 4-0 and things weren't looking good for us. I talked to the player's in-between the periods about the importance of playing with your heart. I said, "What you do here will define you. We don't give up and we don't stop. You have a choice to make. Whoever is not skating will sit. The team needs your best efforts." We started out the third with an energy I haven't seen out of this team. We were on fire and it started with our back checking. The players were confident and playing like it was a 0-0 game. We scored two goals and Matthew didn't let any goals in. We lost 2-4, but we gained a spot to the districts.

Our plan was to pick up the practices and the competition level. We knew we were one of the most competitive teams in the Upper Peninsula. The bigger question was, would our young team be too inexperienced to make it to the next level or, would our talent carry us through? Many of these questions would be answered in the next couple of weeks. This was our second year earning a spot to the districts. It was an accomplishment we could be proud of. I actually thought it would be unattainable due to the negativity that had struck the team all season long.

MOVING FORWARD

I was proud of the team and the performance thus far. I felt anything beyond this point is a bonus. The season was starting to drag on me and I found it harder and harder to find things for practice. I knew the kids were counting on me to do what was right. I just needed some time to concentrate and not be badgered with constant emails degrading the coaches and the players. I decided to block out any and all emails from the parents who were bringing me down and hurting this team. The last email I read was one that told me that the positions the players were in were wrong. Like always his kid didn't have a chance to shine and he is one of the best players on the team. I figured the only way to prove someone wrong or right was to try it out.

Jim disagreed with me about changing the lines and where players were set at, but for my own sanity I decided to try it. Jim felt that I was giving into the cancer and letting him win. I knew what would happen and I wanted to prove him wrong. We had a single game with Park Falls and I had a chance to juggle the lines and see how they would work. I put Baxter and Young on defense paired with CJ and Mitch. I knew our defense would be fine, but I wasn't sure what would happen with the forward offense. Travis would also get some time in net.

The following week January 23, we played Park Falls for only one game. This would be the first and the last time anyone would ever manipulate my team. The players were really surprised on the line change and Jim helped me to sell the idea to the kids. I told them the game didn't count and Travis was in net. Our warm up was like any other. There was nothing different about anything we have done the entire year.

We went to Park Falls with no idea what would happen. We had won most of the games we had played. I was sure of one thing I wasn't going to interfere or change goalies, no matter what the score. My thoughts were not on anything but how we could beat Ontonagon to move on from the districts. Iron River would be tough as well. I figured our team could adapt to anyone else, but the bottom line was Ontonagon was in our heads. No matter what juggling or who we were playing, the focus had remained on the skating.

We lined up for the faceoff and unlike any other game, the players were quiet. I wasn't sure what would happen, but the fact was we were going to find out. The game was an ugly one. We lost 7-10 our offense was nonexistent and our back checking was the worst it had been all year. Park Falls had a goalie that never played before. The high score was indicative that this bright idea was a total failure. It wasn't the lack of preparation or the lack of effort, it was simply the players were not in the right place to make them successful.

After the game I thanked coaches Gerhke and Sturgeon for having us down, and then went to the locker room. I went into the locker room and told the kids that I was proud of them, but the loss was my fault. I let them know I was trying something different to see what would happen since the game meant it was just for fun. The players responded with smiles and they made me feel like it was going to be all right. As I left the locker room the parent who had been complaining was standing in the hall waiting to go in the locker room. I looked him in the eyes and said, "That worked out. Leave the coaching to me. Keep your comments to yourself." He was not happy. I felt much better about my decisions on lines and knew that outside interference is almost always a bad thing.

On the drive home Sarah was mad at me for giving in and changing lines. I didn't know what to say and maybe I lost some respect from the parents, but the season was torture for me. I was not happy about the criticism and the backstabbing. Some of these parents don't want to do the volunteer work but they are more than happy to complain about someone who is doing it. The situation from here on out was going to get better. It was sad to say that I was miserable coaching and I wasn't sure if I would come back the following season. I love coaching more than anything else I do.

The following weekend had a pretty good line up. We were in a 4 team scramble in North Lakeland for an outdoor tournament. We were playing North Lakeland, Stevens Point, and Park Falls and then on Sunday we were playing Ontonagon. I was looking forward to the weekend. I had a practice plan that included two goalies so Travis and Matthew could face one another. I wanted our team to communicate more on the ice. I knew if the players talked that they would better assist each other. Brett and Ethan were doing a solid job on defense since putting them together. CJ and Mitch had been talking already on the ice and Tyler, Warner, and Caleb communicated already. Nathan was a little quiet, but he was smooth on the ice and I think that he was always deep in thought.

On Saturday January 30 we arrived early in a very cold North Lakeland with an intention of enjoying the day playing some round robin tournament hockey. We started out the day against Lakeland with a chilly -15 below. Our pace was not as slow as the weather would dictate. We scored two quick goals in the first minute of the game. Our pace was fast and the cold weather didn't seem to interfere with our gameplay. The second period was a steady back and forth battle, but Lakeland fought back to a 2-2 tie. We went into the locker room and the other coaches and I did our usual corrections to help the team win their individual battles. The mystique of playing outdoors had worn off and we were back to our up and down hockey. This team had so many chances that they didn't capitalize on. The kids took the ice after a quick resurface, reenergized and ready to play. The kids scored 3 unanswered goals and won the game 5-2. Matthew was playing well in net and it was a good sign for the tournament.

The second game was with Price Ice and it was an unusually boring game between us. Most of the time when we hit the ice against Coach Sturgeon's team, it was fast paced and with great passes. However, this game the players on both teams were not hitting their passes or the net with their shots. I think the main reason was that the sun had come out and the reflection off the ice was blinding. The game seemed like it just started when I looked and noticed only a minute was left. I knew that Tyler and Warner were the two go to players that could tie the game since we were down 2-1. Warner won the faceoff and Tyler shot the puck which hit a pipe then went right to CJ's stick. CJ buried the puck and after a short celebration we left the game with a 2-2 tie.

The third and last game was against Stevens Point, Central Wisconsin Saints. They had beaten Price Ice which made this game a championship game. The Saints were a much disciplined team who had a couple of skaters that could flat out fly. The whole day I had been experimenting with shifting players from position to position. I was trying to find some sort of combination of lines where the kids would gel and utilize their hockey skills the best. The game had started and the sun was going down. It was the last game of the day, but it was the most important. For some reason or another, knowing it was a championship game, would make the team perform beyond any of my expectations. We started slower than we had in the previous two games. We were down 1-0 in the first period and I called a huddle on the defensive side of the bench. I asked the players if they were happy with their performance thus far and they all responded "No." I then told them to give 110 percent and no matter what win or lose you leave here all a winner.

Tyler and Warner took much of the leadership on their shoulders and skated with their team to their net to have some motivational team speech. The players were chanting and yelling all together behind the net with their sticks in the air. You could feel that the players were motivated and were going to perform better than they had been playing. The very first shift, Warner took the puck down the ice and buried it in the back of the net. The next shift Nathan Garnell got a nice pass from Brett Heil and he scored a beautiful goal. The goal was one of the nicest I have seen all year long. It seemed that now that we had the lead the players were in their kick back mode. After a few scoring opportunities for the Saints called a time out to settle the players down and get back to business. We went into the third period with a 2 goal lead and momentum on our side. The third period started like the second, fast and great passing. The game went scoreless for the most of the third period but Stevens Point really shot the puck at Matthew. With one minute left Tyler scored an empty netter sealing our victory and our second championship game of the season.

Sunday, January 31 we were at home against Ontonagon. Every time we play them our team brings their best game. The first game we lost 6-3 and Matthew let a few soft goals in. Matthew might have been tired from the three games we played yesterday but I wouldn't make excuses. The team fell apart after Noah Rule scored the 6th goal of the game for Ontonagon. I couldn't motivate or correct some of the team's mistakes. I have always felt that any team I coach should be able to adjust and correct their mistakes. This however, wasn't the case. Our team was tired and it showed. The game had ended and I told the players to relax between games.

Before our second game we had a little chalk talk about how to adjust to adversity with skilled players. Our players are very skilled in the knowledge of the game and the physical abilities they possessed. The problem we have is they were young and not as physically developed as some of the other teams which had much older and larger players. It didn't take very long for the players to understand that use your body as a shield to keep the puck from other players. The coaches also discussed to use angles to catch up to a player that was in front of you. I always hold each player responsible for their mistakes. Mitch had not had a very good game and he seemed a little down after the first game. Tom Kangas spent some time between games talking with Matthew about some of his technical errors that had happened in the earlier game. I talked to him after we were done by the players reassuring him that he was one of our team leaders and this team needed him. I think Mitch was revitalized and had a smile after our short conversation.

Our second game started and the players were focused. The playing field was even. The only advantage we had was that we had one more player on the bench than they did. I made some adjustments by putting Ethan on defense. His skills at this point were stronger on defense than forward. Ethan and Mitch were solid in the game. Matthew had a very solid game by making numerous saves. The players responded, making a very good effort even though we lost 5-3. The kids were proud of their efforts because we had been playing better and better versus Ontonagon. I felt they were the most talented team that we faced that year. The best compliment I can make of our team is every week every player was getting better. Their efforts were not going unnoticed and everyone in the Upper Peninsula knew that this squirt team was a force to be reckoned with.

The growth and development of these kids is crucial, in not only hockey, but other sports as well. I remember telling the players that I wanted to see some of them as all conference in football, basketball, and baseball. I tried to reaffirm that these lessons are taught for them to become those players. The effort is not going to be seen now, but it will be shown in the future. The players really seemed to listen and understand, that the quality of work they put in will show down the road. I think the hardest lesson to teach is the one they don't completely understand. The fact that they believe in themselves and their team was shown by their close knit team play. The story they were writing had been done with blood, sweat, and tears. The season had been dwindling, down but their spirits were still high.

The following week at practice, was time to get back to the basics again. Skating was what got us where we were so that was where we were going. Some players were not giving their best efforts and it showed in games. I needed to make the practices fun and switch some things around to regain the kid's interest. I think as a coach you need to keep your practices flowing and crisp. The sharp play of your kids can transcend into many other aspects of life. The winning attitude is contagious and needs to be spread. As a coach, each of us needs to be very observant to the needs of the team and how to apply that to the individual player.

Friday February 5, we didn't have any games until Sunday and this was a good chance to get ready for districts. I knew we had to skate to get our edges and develop our legs further. I pulled out the power straps and really gave the players a hard work out. The next line of business would be to have a controlled scrimmage to get our positioning and team play sharp. The most important ideas that I have deal with the psyche of each individual player. How do you get the most out of each player and how do you integrate each player to your team concept? I spent lots of time talking with each player and trying to help them to feel that they were a big part of the team. The players needed to feel wanted. It is natural and just human. Each player has positives and negatives and each and every game they show it. The difference is, whether or not you can help that player believe in themselves as much as you believe in them. I try to end each game and practice with some sort of belief speech. I think it is important that they believe it and teams have been successful because they buy into it.

Sunday February 7, we played Ashland, Wisconsin. The players had a great week of practice and we overcame the individual play and concentrated more towards team play. The more advanced players seemed to take the weight of the team from time to time and became selfish to try and do what they thought was best for the team. The first game we came out on fire with great passing and very nice goals by Tyler and CJ. The second period was much of the same. Warner scored 4 goals and Brett assisted on two of them. Brett had become a very nice defenseman making some really nice plays. We won the game 6-2 and Matthew had some really nice saves.

The second game was not as easy, as Ashland didn't give up and they really came at us in this game. Matthew was on today he made some outstanding saves and had a lot of help from Mitch. Mitch got in the offensive part of his game and scored what would eventually be the game winner. We were down 4-1 going into the third period. Between periods I reassured that no team should be overlooked. I thought that the players were looking forward to the districts next week. I lit into the players hoping to motivate and play with a little heart. We hit the ice with a passion that I was very proud of. Caleb had a rough first two periods and was poised to change that. Caleb came out and scored two quick goals assisted by Ethan. Nathan Garnell who was hustling like I had never seen before was making the most of his opportunities. Mitch scored with a minute left and gave us the go ahead 5-4 to seal the win.

Wednesday February 10, I thought that every minute of practice was crucial and needed to be used. We did a lot of passing and some team support play. I also stressed the need of 6 on 5 goalie pulled situations. It is hard to make a game type situation because games are not the same as practice. The effort that I was seeing from time to time in practice was not enough. I am not sure if they were taking it easy on each other or if they were not putting in the effort. I always addressed this aggressively, as I never allow a secondary effort. The emphasis on over speed and technical shooting take time and needed to be done correctly. Sometimes I tried too hard to make sure the drills were done correctly.

My focus on the weekend was to give the players the best chance to win without putting pressure on the players. The parents sometime were too caught up on winning and didn't see the future of their players like I did. I understood the philosophy of winning and that if we are winning the kids are having fun, but there is some disregard to player development. With the thought of the player development not in some parents mind, I needed to remind each parent why the players play the game. Just for the fun of it. The anticipation of districts only two days away was like waiting for Christmas morning to come.

DISTRICTS

Friday February 12, we drove four hours to Manistique who was hosting the district playoffs. Our tournament started off with a really tough draw playing Marquette first. The whole team was ready with Travis Collins. He had stayed home because he was sick. We took the ice and had a really poor warm up. Warner, Tyler and Caleb took their team behind the net for a motivational speech before the game would start. I don't know what they said in the huddle or who even said anything, but you could feel the positive vibes off the kids.

Our first shift was a great indicator of how this game would go. Warner won the face off and Brett passed it to Tyler who then passed it back to Warner to score in the first two minutes of the game. This was the first time I got to see Marquette's team and I was very impressed with their skills. This wasn't going to be a cake walk by any means. The second period went the same as the first with only one goal, scored by Tyler. Between periods, resurface was a needed break by both teams. Our passing was not as good as it had been in previous games, but their speed and hard play was preventing us from getting into a good rhythm.

We hit the ice for the third period and I felt that the players were feeling like they had the game in hand. It took about five minutes, but Marquette scored on a great shot and brought the game within one goal. We needed someone to step it up and give us some breathing room. Nathan Garnell had a sweet goal shortly after I was thinking time was running out and Marquette was getting some nice scoring opportunities. Matthew was playing well and our defense was solid, covering the open man. Caleb

Baxter took the puck coast to coast to score our fourth and final goal. We only had two minutes to kill with a three goal lead. I called a time out to give us a well-deserved rest to help prepare for Marquette's final push. We took back to the ice after the short time out and killed the rest of the time off the clock winning our first game of districts.

After the game we went back to the hotel and had a good meal with the team discussing what we were going to do on Saturday. We were playing Iron River and Iron Mountain, both who we have beaten at least once during the year. The players looked ready and our momentum was positive. I spent a lot of time in our room prepared and thinking of situations that would help with each team. I don't know if I over prepare or if that is what a good coach should do. I just tried to give the players the best advantage they could have to use their skills to make it to the next level.

We woke up early the next morning and went to the rink to watch some games. For any tournament I try to see all the teams playing so I can visualize how to create some miss-matches. We had the second game and there was a very positive vibe in the locker room. The players were singing to the music and we had a lot of positive energy. We took the ice against Iron River. We had played them about 5 or 6 times this year. Right before the drop of the puck I was thinking if we could play like we did yesterday we could propel our team into Sunday's championship round.

Iron River came out to play and unfortunately we didn't. For some unknown reason our whole team didn't pass and it cost us. I think the unique thing with kid's sports is you never know what you are going to get. I tried every motivational technique to help the kids jump start our game. Some players have a bad day but I had never had the whole team do so poorly. I wasn't sure if I had not prepared them enough for the weekend. We wound up losing 4-2 which doesn't sound bad, but the team and I were not happy with our performance.

The thing about being one of the final 8 in the Upper Peninsula was by Saturday night you would know if you had a chance to play to go down state. Saturday night we faced off against Iron Mountain, who we beat 3 times during the regular season. I felt going into the game that we had a great advantage. I knew that if we didn't work hard and win the races to the puck that our weekend could very well be over. Iron Mountain has some very solid players and their skill was comparable to ours.

We took the ice Saturday night with some excitement and some nervousness. Our team had surpassed any expectations that I had before the start of the season. However, with this very young team we had to do the unthinkable. We had to fight out of a hole and we had to win the game or we were not playing on Sunday. The team had made me a believer that they could beat anyone anywhere. I remember standing on the bench thinking how hard the kids had worked and the few negative parents who had made this season a struggle to come back next year.

After a very good warm up and a quick team huddle behind the net, the players came to the bench with smiles and a very positive look. The drop of the puck was moments away and I suddenly became very nervous. My mind started going a million miles a minute. I was hoping that the players couldn't tell that I was nervous. The first period started and we looked like we did earlier that morning. There was no passing at all. The players weren't using their skills. All of the coaches were scrambling on the bench for answers. The first period came to an end and we were down 3-0. It was a horrible hole to try and dig out of. We had our resurface after the first period and it was to our advantage to make some adjustments.

I was searching for answers, but there were none. All of the players had a blank stare on their faces. I only remember telling them to relax and play the game one goal at a time. We had been in the hole before and we had fought back to win those games too. We left the locker room and let the kids listen to some music and get back in the groove. As it is with coaching youth sports and like I have said before, they can be such a big surprise in what they do. I asked Warner when he passed me in the hallway, if they were ready. I still remember Warner saying to me, "We're ready."

We started the second period playing with some energy and heart. We started to win the battles to the puck and in a short time we scored, giving us some badly needed momentum. Warner went to the faceoff and the unthinkable happened. Iron Mountain came right back down and scored. It was like a thief taking your prize possession. I didn't see it coming and neither did our team. The second period was filled with scoring opportunities for both sides and it seemed we couldn't buy a goal. At the end of the second we had pressure but couldn't get the puck in the back of the net. The period ended 4-1.

I called the team together and told them one last time, "You can do this; there is no one here that is as talented as you. Have fun and take this game." I felt that our legs were strong and we still were not passing how I liked. I could only remember Eric Boyer telling me that some games were like quick sand. The more you fight, the deeper you sink. I was hoping for some sort of energy burst but there was none. The third period was very uneventful until I threw a wrench into the mix. With five minutes left, down by three, I knew something needed to be done. We needed goals. I made the decision to pull Matthew to give us the extra skater.

The players hated the idea of the open net. We had worked on some 6 on 5 during the week, but nothing like this pressure. The fact was, if we didn't win we were not going on to Sunday. The second fact was this was a long shot, but to me it was the only one that could help us get back into the game. It wasn't 20 seconds after pulling the goalie that Iron Mountain scored their 5th goal. I think the players were very mad at me for pulling Matthew, but it was the only choice I had. About a minute later we had some pressure on Iron Mountain's goalie, so I pulled Matthew again. As Matthew skated to the bench Iron Mountain took a shot at the empty net and scored their 6th and final goal of the game. As I watched the last second's tick off the clock with a sick feeling of crying players, I watched our team shake hands with Iron Mountain and wish them luck.

I immediately called all the players to the bench holding up the Zamboni because I needed to say something to the players without any parent interference. I said, "You made it to districts. You played your heart out. Keep your head up high because your parents and coaches are very proud of you. Go have fun tonight and see you at practice." I had an empty feeling like I had let them down. The players know what it took to get here and they honestly did the best job that they could. I was still a little disgusted with some of our parents who had some negative comments to say to me and the other coaches.

I went back to the hotel room and didn't come out. I was already preparing for next week's games. I was a little beside myself. I always try to think where and what I could have done differently. The mistakes are not of the player alone. I have to make sure they were prepared. We were definitely the youngest team at districts. I just didn't feel that we as a team gave a good effort. I always take great pride in how awesome our skating is but it wouldn't help us overcome our opponents.

26

A SWEET ENDING

After a long ride home and a few quiet days at work I was ready to end the season and move on. My worst moments as a coach were dealing with parents. The game as a whole can wear on you. Sarah and I had some arguments over some of the negativity which had been pushing me away from the game that I love. Somehow I needed to finish this season and find myself. I was already thinking of walking away for a few years and take a break. Uncertain of what would pull me back to coaching since it had been an extremely stressful year.

Our first practice back on February 17 I invited the mites to come and practice with us for a change of pace. This was the first time I got to see what talent they had and who would be moving up the next season. We had a fantastic practice, almost forgetting about last weekend. At the end of practice we scrimmaged against the girls' team. The scrimmage went well and the mites showed some spunk. After a 30 minute scrimmage we left the ice to find some parents had bought pizza for the team. The season still had a bitter taste in my mouth, but I was going to focus and keep my nose to the grindstone for the rest of the season.

The following weekend we played one game in Park Falls. I put Travis in net to give him an honest shot after more emails degrading certain teammates from our infamous negative parent. I approached the game with a different attitude and told the players to have fun and play hard. I wasn't going to get over excited and the unfortunate thing is I just wanted the season to end. I didn't even check emails any more or messages on my phone.

We took the ice for the first game quieter, than normal. I think the players were catching on to the tensions between some parents. The unfortunate thing is the game is played by the players, but some parents feel they have to interfere. We weren't in the game five minutes and the relentless screaming from that parent. I was beyond embarrassed for our organization to have a classless person even affiliated with us. It was at the point to where that parent had brainwashed his child in such a way that he wouldn't even respond to me talking to him. I told Jim Young, "I don't know what to do for a player who won't even talk to me." To have a player not respond while coaching the others made this stress greater than it had been all season.

The first two periods were sloppy. We gave up 5 goals on 11 shots and were losing 5-2 going into the third period. We were hustling but we were not passing like we should. In the third period those nine year olds came on fire. Tyler and Warner lit Park Falls up for 3 consecutive goals and a ton of momentum going into the last three minutes. The final minute we gambled due to our offensive zone attack and gave up a break away. Seth Gehrke came down the ice and buried it behind Travis. I told Warner we needed a faceoff in their zone. The last minute we didn't get a whistle but, our first line poured it on Park Falls, However failing to score the tying goal. We out hustled them, but we didn't pass well enough to win.

In-between games I asked the parents to have patience with our embarrassment and we only had to endure one more week of the headache. Sarah and I were becoming more and more separated from the team because the negativity was affecting us as well. I knew that not coaching the next season would not do the kids justice. I made the decision in Park Falls that I was going to coach the squirts at least one more season. The talent we had and the hard work we all put in would pay off for each individual player. I couldn't let this cancer take the team over even though I knew the confrontation would be ugly.

I heard some of the derogatory comments made from the stands. My occupation gives me thicker skin than normal, but direct attacks again and again on children, I couldn't stand anymore from this individual. I waited in the hall way and for the first time I didn't give a speech at the end of a game. I asked Jim young to do it because I had to take care of something. I asked the parent to step into the rink for a word. I didn't get two feet in the rink and he pointed his finger in my face telling me what a terrible coach I was. I only said this," You are a shallow man and you have no place in this game. Your attitude and your negativity have destroyed this team. If you ever degrade a child in public or this team I will have you removed from the ice rink. I don't care how much money you have or what you think you know, but you are the reason this team fails. Let the kids play and leave them alone. If I hear one word out of you, I will act on this and have you removed."

I watched him stomp out of the rink to the parking lot. I felt clearly in my mind that the mental growth is being damaged by this negative yelling. I know what I did was right. I stayed in the rink sitting on the bench for a half hour till my heart settled down a little and met Sarah in the concession area. I don't know if anyone heard or saw us talking, but deep down I had to regain control. I knew these kids wouldn't quit and neither would I.

The second game started and I think the players noticed my positive vibes because I noticed theirs. Travis didn't want to go back in net so Matthew got the call. This game was one I couldn't even explain. Our passing was more than outstanding. We had 3 playmakers in the game and won 9-2 Matthew almost got his first shutout of the season but was very solid in net. C.J. made some outstanding passes and shots. Tyler won almost every race to the puck which was the key to helping his teammates. Brett Heil got his first play maker as well as Ethan Roehm. Warner scored 4 goals and Caleb had 2. The game was a great indication that there was no quit in their game no matter what obstacle was in their way.

Wednesday February 24 was our only practice of the week. We had 5 mites come to our practice. There was nothing I could do this late in the season to change skating or hockey skills so I let them scrimmage the full hour. The players had a blast and that's what you would want as a coach and a parent. I had a good feeling about what the weekend would hold for us. Our tournament in Stevens Point would be the highlight of the season.

Friday February 26, our first game of the weekend was against Shaw of Milwaukee. They were a quick team with some solid players. We started like we did our last game, on fire. Matthew made some outstanding saves and got his first shutout of the season as we won 9-0. Tyler was sick with strep throat, but was very solid scoring a couple of goals. Warner had a hat trick and Caleb showed some sweet moves deking the goalie. Nathan was hustling and it showed with a couple of assists. Our defense cleared the crease and Mitch, Brett, Ethan and Baxter had one of the best defensive showings I had ever seen.

Saturday February 27, our second game was versus the home team, Central Wisconsin Saints. I like this team because of their grit. If you play them you know you are in for a fight and they never quit. The game was back and forth the first two periods. Our legs prevailed in the second period winning 5-3. This is by far the roughest game we had all year long. The players were a little sore and I told them after the last game that we could have an hour in the pool, which the kids liked.

In-between games I was in our hotel room and I heard a particular noise in the hallway. It was the sound of kids laughing. I love the sound and make everything I do worth it. The players were having their own tournament, a mini-stick tournament. I wasn't worried about them being too tired because this was their weekend. As our third game became closer I didn't leave the room much. I think I was mentally tired from the season and in the back of my mind I was planning AAA practices.

The third game was against Altoona, Wisconsin. They were a slick little club of 9 players all who hustled. Our game plan going in was simple, keep our passing going and win the race to the puck. Matthew was starting the game and looked really focused. I think going the whole season and coming up short on a shutout was wearing on his mind. C.J. came out with a hot stick scoring two quick goals giving us a 2-0 lead in the 1st period. Altoona came out in the 2nd period firing, but Matthew stoned them and refused to allow a goal. Warner and Caleb had a sweet passing combination that Travis scored on. Up 3-0 going into the 3rd, we came out hustling and looking like they wanted the championship. Brett and Ethan scored giving us the 5-0 lead and helping Matthew to his 2nd shutout of the year. We normally didn't play well, but today the kids looked focused.

We were in the semifinals later Saturday afternoon when we played Tomahawk, Wisconsin. The team was raring and ready to go. They were unusually quiet, but it was a focused quiet. They knew if they were to win they would go on to the championship game. Tyler, who was sick, had one of his best games of the year. He had a goal and two assists, accompanied by some sweet passing. Nathan scored on one and was hustling big-time. Travis had some nice back checking that helped score our second goal. Brett and Ethan were solid on defense helping Matthew keep the door closed on Tomahawk. We won the game 3-0 propelling us into the championship game. Matthew had earned, an unbelievable 3rd shutout for the weekend.

The parents were really happy about how the kids were performing and they were having fun doing it. The families all put together a pot luck dinner that was very impressive. The players were either swimming or they were playing floor hockey. I walked by some rooms and even watched some video games being played by a few younger brothers and sisters. This was the team I wanted, one that gets along and one that works hard for each other. I was not sure if we would win the championship, but bonding the players were doing made it well worth doing what I do.

Sunday February 28, we were playing the Central Wisconsin Saints, the home team in the championship game. I was excited and a little nervous. The players who had a fun filled weekend had worked for this chance to win. We hit the ice running and scored first. Brett Heil shot one high glove side. Central Wisconsin came right back and scored right away. Later in the first period Central Wisconsin scored two more to put us down 3-1. The second didn't start any better. The Saints scored in the first minute and the blood was in the water. Down 4-1 I called a time out to slow their momentum. I couldn't believe we were down because we were actually playing really well. The Saint's goalie made some key stops on Warner and Tyler especially. After the time out we came out scoring. Brett scored two goals and Ethan scored one right before the intermission, making it 4-4 going into the third. In the locker room I told the players that they were already winners, and to keep their heads held high. I told them," If you keep working good things will happen."

We took the ice in the third with an uncertainty. The game was up for grabs and the next goal could be the one who wins the game. I knew our legs were ready but the Saints came to play and they were focused. It was a back and forth 3rd period. About five minutes in the Saints struck. It was a very nice goal from one of their defensemen. Matthew was screened and it was a good goal. I was a little worried because I had no time outs left and we were down. Mitch gave a pass to Caleb who brought it up the ice and hit the post. You could hear the fans gasp, and then out of nowhere came Ethan Roehm and shot the puck to the back of the net with two minutes left.

The Saints called a time out and gave me the time I needed to try and put something together. I knew their best would be out the next shift so I line matched them with our best defensive group. Warner, Tyler and Caleb would match any speed they would have and we might even score with those players out on the ice. Mitch and CJ on defense to give us the size we would need to clear the net. However, what I was thinking, "Who could score on the second line?" because I was going to double shift who ever had enough energy left. As it would play out we had the scoring opportunities, but the strongest line I could put out was tired and there was 30 seconds left. Brett skated one up along the boards and broke free and took a shot with 15 seconds left. The Saints goalie made a great stop and Nathan Garnell shot the puck back and scored the game winner.

The team showed that they never quit and I was very proud of them. We had one more tournament next week but I was ready to end the season on this note. We were going to Iron River to play. As it played out Iron River would be going to the state tournament in two weeks. They were doing well and playing their best hockey before the tournament. I didn't look at emails that week because I just wanted it to end. I really love the game but it was wearing on me.

We had our normal practice on Wednesday and I did the same as I had been doing for practice. I really like ending a season on a good note and I was fearful that we wouldn't have that happen with all the drama caused by some parents. This was our last practice and I don't think I blew a whistle. The kids had a blast and we ended the practice with some pizza. I received the trophies on Thursday. Like Sarah and I do every year we get the kids trophies and I was going to pass them out at the rink on Sunday. We usually do a party a few weeks later but due to the ugliness of this past season I chose not to.

We went to Iron River on Friday playing the home team. Our team started the game very slow. We didn't win the race to the puck or make the passes like we did a week earlier. There wasn't much to say other than every positive aspect of our game had disappeared. We lost 3-0 and Iron River deserved to win that game. Our friend got us a room so Sarah and I stayed at another hotel because I couldn't be around the negative parent any longer. It was sad that I dreaded the next two days because of one person who had made my coaching experience miserable.

On Saturday I woke up early, as I always do, and did my normal game preparations. There was some sadness coming over me that the season was ending soon, but for my mental state and the solidarity, some of the parents it needed to be over. We were playing a tough Newberry team with some very nice skaters on their squad. The kids looked refreshed and ready to play. Our warm up was the best it had been all season long. We came out in the first period passing and shooting. We scored six goals in the first period and Newberry could only muster one. We went to the second period with a renewed confidence. Each player had managed to get a point by the end of the second and we were up 9-1. I told the player's in-between the second and third periods, to keep focused and work on their passing. I didn't want to run the score up but at the same time I didn't want to let go of this momentum we had found. The end score was 11-1 and we were playing K-Bay in a few hours.

I thought about the natural way the players looked. Especially our first year skaters. It seemed like every team but ours was carried by their second year players. I wondered if next season there would be a team to emerge with some fantastic first year players or would they have some diamond in the rough surprising everyone. Only time would tell. The parents were already talking about the thought of playing next season.

Later Saturday afternoon we played K-Bay and like the last game, the kids were very happy. I noticed our warm up wasn't as crisp as it was in the morning. I was thinking the kids had become content with their efforts thus far. We came out in the first period and got out played. K-Bay had a quick 2-0 lead. The period came to an end and I asked the players if they were happy with their performance thus far. All the players looked disappointed and said, "No". I then told the kids to forget about the first period and let's play some Polar Bear hockey. Pass the puck and go have fun. The players seemed to respond to our non-urgency to win games or score goals. I always try to validate that winning is not important, but playing your best is.

We started the second period like we did the entire first game. We came back led by Caleb's quick goal with a great assist from Brett and CJ. Warner and Tyler then lit the lamp about a minute later to tie the game at 2. I was very proud of my Polar Bears for giving their best efforts. Right before the end of the second K-Bay had a breakaway and made a great move to beat our defensemen, scoring the third goal on a nice deke. In-between the second and third I didn't have a whole lot to say. I walked into the locker room and sat down. Each player looked very tired. I think the emotional roller coaster each competitor puts on themselves can be very hard at times. I reminded each player that they wouldn't remember who won this game but they would remember that they didn't quit.

We took the ice in the third very quiet. There wasn't much talking and I wasn't sure what to make of it. The players came out firing. We spent the first half in K-Bays zone. K-Bay's goalie was making some phenomenal stops. Towards the last six minutes Warner scored the game tying goal on a sweet Garnell assist. The speed and momentum was in our favor but the game was far from over. K-Bay came back firing the last five minutes and we looked tired. I was hoping we could hold them off. K-Bay had two consecutive breakaways which Matthew made some great saves on. I called a time out to settle us down and give us a break. If a goalie is playing as well as Matthew was, I didn't want to shake his confidence and just gave him a quick compliment. We gave the players some water for the final minute of play. The last minute was very uneventful, both teams kept the puck safe in the neutral zone and the game ended in a 3-3 tie.

As I left the locker room to see how the points played out I was met by Sarah. She was smiling ear to ear saying we made it to the championship game on Sunday. I returned to the locker room and informed the team that their hard work had propelled them into the championship game against Iron River. Sarah and I went back to the hotel room and watched, what else, an NHL game. We went down to the dining room and had dinner with the Heils and the Clemens. I didn't do any preparing that night. I just wanted the kids to do what they could. They had played very well with the first game being the only exception.

Sunday morning I slept in later than I normally did. I was hoping to get to the rink and finish the season up with some dignity. Iron River was preparing to go down state the following Friday to play for a state championship. Two things you could count on with Iron River, one, they are much disciplined and two their goalie played very well against us.

We came back to the rink and the players seemed very nervous. Jim Young and I were out in the lobby with Brian Roehm and we let them listen to some music and we would just go get them when the ice was ready.

Iron River went out on the ice first. I walked back to a locker room full of singing players. I cracked a smile and asked them one last time, "ARE YOU READY!" in a loud voice. The players responded "YES" and hit the ice running. They were ready and maybe we could pull a great upset.

Warner took the faceoff to start the game like he did with most games. Tyler and Nathan were his wings. The puck dropped and the game was on. I couldn't believe that we went almost 6 minutes without a whistle. Each team was changing on the fly and up and down the ice we went. Before you knew it the first period was over tied 0-0. It was very exciting and the player's legs on both teams looked strong. There wasn't much to say other than words of confidence. Jim was excited and so was Tom Kangas. We faced off in the second period and our defensive side of the game was outstanding. Ethan, CJ, Brett and Mitch were playing very solid in front of Matthew, blocking shots every chance they could. All 13 players were moving the puck very well and everyone had a scoring opportunity in one way or another.

The second period came to an end with the same score as the first. A game with not much offense was a truly awesome display of grit and skill on both sides of the puck. Both teams weren't slowing down. It was a fast paced game and our first year players were standing up to their second year players. The practices and the learning were showing. I didn't even think of a negative thing that was said by anyone for once. I told the players, "We are a team, a solid team, age doesn't matter but the fact that each of you came to play is an awesome display." I told them that each of their parents were proud of them and to finish as strong as they started. "There is no quit in this team, work your hearts out and play to the whistle."

The third period started and I was getting a little nervous. Iron River looked energized and I looked forward to a great period. Warner took the faceoff and Tyler skated the puck up the left side of the ice and took a shot. The puck slammed off the cross bar. It was close but it didn't go in. We kept the puck in the zone and CJ took a shot which hit the pipe as well. It made a loud ping that could be heard throughout the rink. The puck went to an Iron River players stick and off to the races. It was a breakaway with two minutes left. He came down with a great amount of speed. He made a great deke and beat Matthew. It was probably the best deke I had seen all year long. There was an emptiness that overtook me. It felt like I was punched in the stomach.

I called a time out shortly after with about a minute left. The players were teary eyed and looked like their worlds had ended. I remember telling them," It isn't over. There is no quit. Play till the end and be proud of what you have done. But we aren't done. Give one last push." I put all of our hands together in a huddle and all counted, "one, two, three, Polar Bears." I pulled Matthew to give us another skater. I set the play up to give us a great scoring opportunity.

Warner took the faceoff and Tyler was the shooter on the left offensive zone circle. The play worked out excellent. The puck went over the net and Iron River attempted to ice the puck with Mitch holding the puck in. The next 60 seconds felt like an eternity. With 10 seconds left we had the puck in the crease and made every attempt to hit the back of the net, but an Iron River defenseman made an excellent play to clear the puck and complete the game. After we shook hands and received our second place trophy we went in the locker room. I got all the parents in the locker room and handed out individual trophies like we do every season. I did this as quickly as I could and before anyone could notice I slipped out the back door of the locker room and Sarah and I headed home. The season was complete. I did it with as much class and toleration as I could muster. It felt like a great weight had been lifted off my shoulders.

The next morning I had to work and I felt that I had let down some of my players. They practiced hard and played even harder just to see some parents ruin it. It felt like my job wasn't done. I had a vacant feeling because I didn't communicate with every player. The last month and a half had been torture because a player refused to talk to me or communicate in any way. I needed to put the season and all of its negativity behind me.

27

SUMMER FUN

After a few relaxing weeks had passed I went to Milwaukee for another Tundra AAA tournament. I couldn't stay all weekend because I had to be in Lakeland for tryouts. The 2000's were my favorite group to coach because I have watched most of these players grow and develop. Tim Gehrke and Jim Young were helping me on the bench for the weekend. We arrived at the rink with some of the kids in awe at the size of the speed skating rink. I liked this tournament because it always had different teams that we wouldn't see in the winter. I think the kids who play summer hockey are ready for the sacrifice to work as hard as it takes to be successful.

Saturday morning we played Milwaukee and won. It was a great thing because some of the players, like Rease Hubert and Hank Bailey, were playing on this team. The dexterity between players gives me a vision at times on how each player can complement another. CJ did really well also, scoring his first hat trick of the year. This was very impressive since he didn't do it all season long. The second game went well, beating Chicago 4-1. It was an impressive start and we needed to keep up the good work.

Early the next morning I had to leave to make the tryout in Lakeland on time. I got the players together at the hotel and told them how proud I was of them and that we needed to kick it up a notch. I said goodbye to some of the parents and headed north. After a few hours Sarah and I arrived at the rink a little early so Eric and I could discuss what we were looking for.

It was nice to see some familiar faces and some new ones. We had our tryout which lasted about three hours total. The players did really well and it was incredible to see how much improvement each player had made. Brandon Hunt was the first person I saw enters the locker room. Sam Lehman and Zach Kennedy walked in next. Seeing the familiar faces helped me to appreciate coaching again. We hit the ice with some new faces as well. Brady Guilbault had come from Ontonagon. It wasn't five minutes and I was in Brady's ear about giving his best effort and how it would help him to become a better player.

At the end of the tryouts Sarah and I went back home and discussed at length about who performed and who didn't. I found that Sarah's views and mine differed, but overall she had a good eye for talent. The only thing that sucks about tryouts is that you have to ruin some kids day by telling his parents that they didn't perform up to standards. After that unpleasant deal is done, and then the true summer season begins.

Both teams I was involved with the, 96's and 00's both had some nice talent. The summer would have some great ups and down for each team. The practices were on Saturdays and back to back to agree with my work schedule. It was busy with six hours of practice on the ice. It was tough on the body but it was well worth it for the players. To plan a AAA practice is opposite of what you do in the summer. I try to teach the kids systems that complement their talents to help them achieve success.

The summer holds many curves when it comes to playing at an elevated level. There are some teams that are very talented as a whole, and there are some that have individuals that are stellar. Coaching the blizzards AAA organization was an honor and I treated it as such, giving my best efforts as well. The players seem to excel and bring something special to their regular season teams after playing in their summer season.

The AAA teams play in five tournaments each and I would only be able to make six of the ten tournaments. I found that being so busy helped this summer go by so fast that the next moment it seemed like we were at the ICUP in Blaine, Minnesota and it was over. Each team had done really well and won a few tournaments along the way. I had one big memory of the summer and it came on a Sunday in May. I was at the 96's home tournament and we just had taken second place when I received a call from one of my parents on the 00' team. They were in the championship game of the Cheese Cup in Green Bay. I wanted to go down but I wasn't sure about how long it would take to get there. Eric's daughter Emma was playing and his wife Barb was already there. Eric was going and Sarah and I tagged along. Eric wanted us to take his truck back because he would drive back with Barb. We made it down so I could be on the bench with the 00's and Eric could watch Emma. We were playing a very tough team and they had not lost all weekend long. Tyler and the rest of the Blizzards were anxious to get to action.

The First period was owned by the Blizzards with Tyler Hunt scoring on a very nice shot assisted by Sammy Spencer. Towards the end Tyler Morrison assisted Brenden Hoover's backhand that found the back of the net. The Blue Devils came out in the second period and put it to us. They scored 3 unanswered goals and were scoring at will. We had a short intermission while they resurfaced the ice. The team started the third a little like they did the first. We came out fast and with a purpose. Tyler Morrison scored in the first minute of the third, tying the game. About a minute later Caleb Baxter scored on a Hank Bailey assist to give us the lead. The Blue Devils came back hard and fast but our defense was tough and wouldn't let any easy goals. The Blue Devils with a minute left, pulled their goalie attempting to put another goal on the board, but Hank Bailey carried one up out of the zone and scored to seal the win and the tournament for the young 00' Blizzards.

Sarah and I met the Boyer's out for dinner after the game and discussed our win and how the summer was shaping up. Eric felt that each player had grown and I agreed with him. It was unfortunate that the summer was so short, because you do grow close to the families and the players. As we left Green Bay I had been thinking of what would happen the following season and how excited I was about the team we would put on the ice.

28

BAD NEWS

I went to work the following day and found out some devastating news. Jim Young who was an Assistant Deputy Warden was informed that his job was being discontinued and he would be forced to relocate to Newberry. I was devastated. Not because we were losing Jim from work or Warner off our team, but because I was losing my friends. Gabrielle, James, and Warner were not only players but they were friends as well. It felt like someone died. I hated the feeling of someone losing their job first of all, but to be forced to move was an unhappy thing.

I went home and told Sarah about what was going on with the Young's. She was not happy and had many questions. No answer was the right one however. It simply was Jim was moving and so was the family. I wasn't worried about the kids playing or not playing. I was worried about how they all would feel. Jim was confident that he would be doing a lot of traveling to keep the kids involved in whatever sports they would like to play. I wasn't sure how to take the news because it deeply depressed me. If any one of my players moves it devastates me.

I had been coaching Warner for four years and saw incredible growth, not only in him, but the players he influenced as well. Gabrielle whom I have coached as well was starting to develop into a great athlete and I knew she would contribute no matter where she would go. James was a dedicated physical fitness guru. Jimmy would be fine on any team and be a leader. As for the only one that lost, was our team. Not only did we lose a captain and our team leader in points, but we lost a friend. The questions about the season were already starting. Would our team be able to recover from that sort of loss or would one or more players stand up and make a triumphant statement. Time would tell.

The next few weeks I helped Jim with some moving. I was always hopeful that they would return and our original team would be renewed. Our team wouldn't go off track and we would push on, but it did hurt losing a player like Warner. The last time I would see the Young's would be to help them move some items to their storage garage. We left with final hugs and a tearful wave good-bye.

LAYING THE FOUNDATION

I knew the Young's move would wear on me because, I do get close to the players and I already knew who would step up. I had to establish some building blocks and develop a plan to pull this team together. The building blocks had to be established from our own players that were developed right here. I knew that we had a ton of talent and most teams didn't match up against us. For once this team had more second year players on it and we didn't have to move anyone up due to our lack of numbers. The first building block was a solid foundation. I wanted the best coaching they could get and I started there. Brian Roehm, Bob Heil, Tom Kangas all agreed to be on the bench with me.

The next line would be to find student coaches. The student coaches play a very direct affect to the support the players need. It also gives them mentors that they can grow to look up to. I asked Jonathan Clemens because of his nice skills and because he was generally a good kid who I could count on. I then asked Justin Niemi to help out. Justin agreed and would be a valuable help with his dedication and great speed. I asked Jacob Baxter who was a goalie and it would give us a goalie that Matthew could learn from. I was approached by Andy Templar. Andy was a senior and he was great with the kids. I think the kids looked up to Andy more than any other player. The last line of the foundation would be the foundation of the team, the captains.

I talked to Caleb first, about being captain, and asking if he could help lead this team. Caleb looked at me with his one of a kind smile and said,

"I can do it." I then told him that I was going to ask Tyler and C.J. if they would like to be co-captains with him. Caleb said, "Awesome." I talked to C.J. next. I asked C.J. if he would like to be captain. C.J. responded," Sure." C.J. was not a talkative kid but he gave every effort and was very coachable. I tried to joke with him and asked if he didn't want to I could find someone else. C.J. just shrugged his shoulders with his sinister smile on his face. I walked away thinking that each one of these kids were one of a kind and they were so special in their own way.

I finally went to Tyler and asked him one question. "Tyler, can you lead this team and do what it takes to help us through the good times and the bad?" Tyler responded," Yes, I can do that." Tyler then said one thing I will never forget. "What are we going to do? What are lines going to be?" I responded, "I'm not sure what we will do, but I know whatever it is we will succeed." Tyler looked at me with a huge grin on and said, "We can do anything." I knew right there that we would be alright. I knew that not only those three would be leaders on this team but there were a few others that could do the same if asked.

C.J., Caleb and Tyler were looking at their 3rd and final year of squirts. Each player had developed into very nice hockey players. It took a lot of belief with their parents and dedication to their players to help them to develop at such an advanced stage. I felt the extra year of squirts would not only help them to develop further but it would help them become better teammates as well. I thought it would also give them a leadership quality that every team needs.

We still didn't have signups for a few weeks but I was looking forward to getting the players focused and ready to play. We needed to get their minds and their bodies ready for the long season in front of us. In seasons past I had always tried to give the players goals. Not too high, but goals they could achieve. Instead, this year, there were no goals. My only goal was to keep the practices fun and challenging. I wanted them to have fun and enjoy their time on the ice. I wanted them to learn whatever our coaches and student coaches could teach as well.

30

THE DRY SEASON

I tried to keep things the same, as in years past by having dry land training and get the players involved. I emailed all the parents. I was surprised at the great response in wanting to do dry land training. It was apparent that these kids were ready to go and wanted to perform. It was a good feeling that each player who showed up was ready and willing to do everything necessary to become a better player. We tried to make dry land training fun and active for each player. We worked on individual stretching and footwork. There was a great emphasis on jumping and speed work.

I deeply researched all physical training for each age group and adapted them for the safest training we could do. Muscle development differs but the physiology doesn't. The main thing was to keep them active and hydrated as much as possible. Flexibility was emphasized, along with a good duration of repetition. The cycles we created seemed to work because the players were not only fatigued, but they were developing their coordination. This is where they began to get the idea of personal sacrifice. The team was learning how to be a team and what that means. Their closeness would only get better once the season began.

I think the most important part of a team is chemistry. One, they have to get along. Two, they have to work hard for each other. And last, they have to have self-sacrifice to help the team get better as a whole. We were meeting three times a week in October to get ready for the ice. I pushed the players harder and harder to see how far they could push their young bodies. Brian and Jeff Baxter assisted a ton and had awesome ideas of their own, which we would install into our dry land training exercises.

Jacob Baxter had been coming to our dry land to get ready for his upcoming Bantam season. Justin Niemi and Jonny Clemens were participating to prepare for their Bantam season as well. Our Bantams were thinking of combining with Ontonagon's Bantams due to our short numbers. There was a board meeting after our registration on September 5. Our existence depended on what Ontonagon wanted to do.

After our registration I knew our team was set. We would have three new players added to our already solid team. Sydnee Lorenson, Tommy Lundin, and David Collins would move up to our Squirt team. Our returning players were Tyler Morrison, Caleb Baxter, CJ Sorensen, Matthew Clemens, Travis Collins, Brett Heil, Ethan Roehm, Nathan Garnell, and Hanna Koivisto. This team had every talent imaginable. Their heart and dedication was without question. I knew I would have to be flawless in the design of our lines and the execution of our team's direction. We also had 7 total coaches on the roster, so we wouldn't miss anything.

The Bantams didn't fare so well at registrations. We only had four sign up and one was a first year player. They were Justin Niemi, Jonathan Clemens, Andrew Danielson, and Delaina Pierce. We immediately got a hold of Dave Guilbault who was coaching the Ontonagon team. Their numbers were down as well, but there was one common problem. No Goalie. I asked Jeff Baxter if Jacob would like to play for the combined Bantam team. It took a few days to decide but it would be a decision he wouldn't regret. The combined team, along with Jacob, would be a nice compliment. Adam asked if I would help with practices and I agreed.

October seemed to fly with all of the dry land we were doing and I was preparing for two teams this season instead of one. I knew it would be a big responsibility but it was one that I welcomed. I hadn't had the chance to coach Andrew, Justin, or Jonny for a few years so I was looking forward to that. I also knew that the combination of the talent Ontonagon was brining and the talent we had, could be a great combination. I wasn't sure how it would play out, but I knew it would be fun watching.

The first and foremost responsibility was the squirts. We needed to make a few changes from last season to help the team perform better. We had been working on certain drills that would conform our team into better skaters and help further their skills by challenging them. We also needed to keep the information about nutrition and hydration fresh in their minds. The last thing was to have practices at a good time so they could get enough rest to recover.

We had one last board meeting towards the end of October so we could establish practice times and to ensure everyone's ice time would be fair. Last year we took Friday practices, but we needed to get rid of that time slot due to our team not having enough time to recover. We checked out what the best times were and came up with a schedule. The Squirts would go from 7:30-8:30 on Mondays and would split with the Bantams on Wednesdays from 630-7:30. We would also have an optional practice Thursday with the Bantams from 4:00-5:00. It was great splitting ice. It was an advantage that would benefit both teams.

31

❧◆❧

GAME TIME

After a great dry land pre-season, both teams were ready to start practice and get ready for the upcoming games. I will never forget that first practice we had that 2010-2011 season. Our squirts were filled with smiles and the anxiety of games was on each and every person's mind. I knew I needed to put together practices that were fun and a little different. As for the Bantams, I wanted to focus on getting them ready for the next step by increasing their skills and their hockey sense. I had been working on practice plans thanks to Jeff Baxter who had a USA hockey practice plan DVD. I knew I could use this since it had drills for each age group.

It took a good week to get assembled what I was going to do and how I would approach each team. I knew with the squirts that we were going to be fine since we had coached together before, but for the Bantams, I was wondering how I would do it without stepping on toes. Adam and Dave were their coaches and I would just overlook their hockey skills. Our first practice in Ontonagon went incredibly well and Dave ran a nice practice. When it came time I would talk to Dave about what I would teach them and how it would benefit them in their future endeavors.

After being a part of some great practices, I was relieved after having such a terrible last season, that this one was shaping up to be one of the best of my coaching career. It was what I needed to help keep me coaching. The squirts were craving games. I think they were chomping at the bit to get to those games more than I was. Bob Heil said to me at one of our practices," anything less than the UP Finals are not acceptable. We have a

134

ton of talent." I just told Bob that we would do the best we could. It was a great pressure with high expectations of how the players would respond to game situations.

Each of our practices in November was spot on. The challenges were taken in stride. Each player was trying harder than they had in previous practices. The bantams were taking a while to gel, I think they were thinking too much and not flowing. I knew it would take time and we had plenty of time till the play downs. I wasn't worried about how they would play because after all, that is why they are here.

It wasn't long until we started our games and we were a week away from Thanksgiving. The following weekend we had our first games of the year versus Ashland, Wisconsin. I still needed to work on our hustle. It looked good in practice and our passing looked outstanding, but I wasn't sure how we would match up against some teams who were solid throughout their roster. I focused that week on back checking and winning races to the puck. This caused some tension amongst our team since they were already ultra-competitive.

Our last practice on Wednesday I wanted to work their legs as much as I could. I would have our situations in the middle of practice, doing some 3 on 2's, but eventually doing some small games that our team liked to do. The flow of our practices was excellent and the players, who I had been driving like a bunch of sled dogs, were focused and looked better than any team I had coached before. After the practice one of our parents had bought Pizza for our team. It was a nice gesture and the kids sure appreciated it.

I was at work for Thanksgiving and I was still thinking about our games in a few days. I was doodling with lines and situations. Like always I sometimes overthink what may and may not happen. I have always tried to be totally prepared for what may come. When I got home that night I set our lines for the last time, making sure our offensive and defensive coverages were even. I was happy with the way it looked on paper, but I was sure I would have to make some adjustments.

November 28, our first games of the new season. We were playing Ashland in their home rink. I wanted to start some kind of habit before games, I made sure I went and had a good breakfast every morning of games. I thought it would be an excellent way to start the day and help to show the players that nutrition is very important. I had a good breakfast and Sarah and I drove to Ashland to get our season under way. I was a little nervous driving there, having some deep thoughts of what we would do in the game. I also was thinking of each player and where they wanted to play and how they could best assist their team.

32

DROP THE PUCK

Every year I let the players listen to music in the locker room before the game. I believe it takes their minds off the pressures they may feel and creates some team comradery. I remember walking into the locker room with the players singing a song and really enjoying their time. I always stop the music, give the lines, and let them be until it is time to hit the ice.

I announced the lines that coaches Heil, Roehm and myself decided on. First line was Morrison at center, Garnell on wing, and Koivisto on the other wing. Second line would be Roehm at center, Baxter at wing, and D.Collins at wing, With Lorensen switching with Koivisto and D. Collins. Our defensive pair would be Heil and Lundin. The other pair would be Sorensen and Travis Collins. I was confident about what we could accomplish as a balanced offensive and defensive team. I went into the hallway and thought about what the game would bring to our team.

I started thinking that our practices were the best I had ever seen out of any team that I had coached. But I knew it wouldn't be easy losing our top scorer who would have been on this team. How would our captains lead this team? There were so many questions I had and the season would provide the answers. I knew that our team would only be as good as our weakest link. It was time the referees were on the ice and I entered the locker room and hollered, "ARE YOU READY!" the kids all stood up and yelled back, "YEAH!" I then backed up and the kids hit the ice. I walked across the ice with Bob and Brian to the bench ready to start another fun filled season.

The players finished their warm up and the captains went to the Ashland bench to shake the coaches' hands to wish them luck. Tyler's line was starting and Ethan's was second. Ashland played the national anthem and the players went behind the net for one last pep talk before the game.

Tyler glided to the faceoff with a solid confidence. Nathan was at his right wing, Hanna at his left. Tommy Lundin and CJ started on defense. The referee looked at both goalies with his hand held high in the air waiting for the goalies to respond that they were ready. Matthew held his catcher glove high in the air and Ashland's goalie did the same. The referee dropped the puck and Tyler won it clean to CJ. CJ skated it up and dumped it in the Ashland offensive zone. Nathan skated hard to the corner and began to scrum with an Ashland defensemen. Tyler was giving good puck support and received a pass from Nathan. Tyler quickly shot to a high corner and scored with only a 1:09 into the game.

The second line came out with Caleb at wing and Sydnee centered by Ethan. The passing off the faceoff was breathtaking. Ethan won the faceoff and it went to Brett who passed it to Caleb as he was streaking down the left wing. Caleb skated as hard as he could and got past the Ashland defensemen. Caleb shot an awesome backhand and put it up over the goalies left shoulder making it 2-0 with only 1:25 in the game!

Ethan took the faceoff again, but this time Ashland won it to their wing and shot it in our zone. Travis went back to get the puck and lost it in a scrum. Caleb came off the high side and took the puck away before the Ashland forward could get a shot. Caleb made a perfect pass to Ethan between the defensemen. Ethan skated the breakaway down and shot it past the Ashland goalie to make it 3-0.

The next couple of shifts were even, but we continued to pressure the Ashland goalie. About 4 minutes later we went on the power play and Tyler scored his second goal of the game assisted from Sydnee. On the next faceoff the Ashland center took the puck down and scored on 11 seconds later. The game was 4-1 and Ashland was showing signs of life. You could feel the momentum swinging and we needed to slow them down and stop it.

Tyler scored two minutes later assisted from Nathan and Brett, for his first hat trick of the season and giving us the 5-1 lead. It was a minute later and Ashland showed some really nice passing and shot a back door goal to make the game 5-2. The first period ended and I was very pleased that we hustled the entire period. I thought our defense got bored and it showed with only 5 shots and two goals. We were starting the second period on the power play due to an Ashland player getting a penalty towards the end of the first.

I told Tyler that the next goal, I was going to switch him to defense and work strictly on passing, so if he were going to get it to make it quick so we could work on the rest of the team. Tyler wasn't too keen on the idea, but he rarely complained and went to the faceoff circle. Tyler pushed the puck past Ashland's center and skated straight down the ice scoring from the top of the circles only 7 seconds in, assisted from Nate and Brett again. Nathan and Brett had achieved their playmakers which to me is a greater achievement than scoring goals.

Caleb scored 1:27 in, assisted from Ethan and CJ. The game was now 7-2 and we were starting to pull away. I don't ever want to bury or embarrass a team so I was preparing to set up new lines and work on passing and getting other players some opportunities. Caleb scored another goal two minutes later assisted by Ethan and Brett. Caleb got his hat trick and Ethan and Brett scored their playmakers. I immediately changed lines by putting Nathan, Caleb, Tyler and Ethan on defense. The rule was they weren't allowed to score any more goals but they could make passes to those who could.

It took about two minutes, but Brett scored his first goal of the year assisted by Tyler and Caleb then CJ scored 20 seconds later with assists by Tyler and Ethan. It was starting to seem like Ashland was frustrated and didn't want to play anymore. I couldn't blame them. They were a young team with a lot of potential. I had to keep making rules to challenge my team and make it nearly impossible to score any more goals at 10-2. I felt the game was in hand, but most importantly to teach the kids some sportsmanship.

Ashland came out a few minutes later and scored on back to back shifts making it 10-4. The rest of the period we controlled the puck and made some incredible passes. Travis, Hanna, David, Tommy and Sydnee had some great scoring opportunities, but most importantly, their on ice communication was getting better and better each shift. The second year players really embraced listening and keeping focused. The third period there was no scoring on either side, but we continued to pass the puck on running time and control the period.

I sat with Sarah between games and had a very good discussion about how our team had progressed and looked really solid. Sarah was very pleased with our passing and unselfishness. We had almost two assists for every goal. I was happy with our team speed. I wasn't particularly happy with some of our defensive zone. I felt we were too worried about scoring and not getting the puck out of the zone. Ashland had only 10 total shots on goal and scored on 4 of them. I knew Matthew was getting bored because he would only face a shot once every three minutes.

The second game was much the same as the first. We scored 8 goals in the first period to Ashland's 1. I pulled the same players back to defense and they didn't disappoint. Ashland only got off 7 shots the entire game. Hanna, Tommy, David and Sydnee all scored their first goals of the season. Nathan showed a bunch of promise at defense and did really well on the penalty kill. David Collins was a nice surprise on the penalty kill with Tyler assisting. The game had ended 13-3 and we started the season 2-0.

I knew what we had to work on in practice. I knew that the team was always going to have our bread and butter drills. The drills were going to be at each and every practice. Skating is the most important part of their age development. My attention was strictly on the player's skills and psyche. I felt we were confident, but not over confident. The coaches were constantly telling the players that we were a good team, but not a great team.......yet.

I wanted to keep challenging the kids and attempting to push them to their limits at each and every practice. I wanted to challenge some of our better skaters against our lesser talented skaters. I found this sometimes to be very unfruitful. Some of the players were still too young and failed to try and beat a teammate in a race. Some players it didn't matter. They wanted to win every race no matter if it was one of the best skaters against them. The coaches strived to push each player to their utmost potential. Tom Kangas was working hard with Matthew to keep him focused even when we had the game in hand.

The team had an excellent week of practices and they were ready for more competition. We were playing Negaunee next, who in the past, had really pounded my Polar Bear teams. There was always a tough group of players there. I was anxious to see how they would do this season since we improved and our team speed was the best it had ever been.

We entered Negaunee which was snow covered on the Friday before our game. We went up a night early to go see a college game and to let the kids tour Northern Michigan Universities' locker room after the game. The team got to see a great game which northern unfortunately lost, to Miami of Ohio. The players were so excited to see the fast paced energy that collegiate hockey brings. I was watching the game as closely as I could so I could use some of their plays in one of our game.

After the game I stood outside Northern's locker room waiting for my players to come out, I saw each Polar Bear come out with an unforgettable grin. I had such a pleasing feeling that comes when the kids are having one of those experiences that I had when I was a kid. We exited the arena and headed to the hotel. I really didn't know what to expect the next morning but our team was working hard and adapting really well. Negaunee has two teams, OK Industrial and Ishpeming Concrete. We were playing Ok Industrial.

We hit the ice early and it seemed all the players prepared for the game by getting a lot of sleep. However, our warm up was a little slow. Bob and Brian agreed that our team wasn't looking real crisp. The thing about kids is, you never know what you are going to see out of them. Tyler took the faceoff and immediately took the puck down to Negaunee's zone and had a couple of quick shots. Negaunee's goalie was doing outstanding and we had a ton of pressure the first couple of shifts.

Tyler finally scored with an assist from CJ on a sweet shot from the slot. Negaunee had back to back break away on us but Matthew stoned them cold and looked really good. The game could have gone either way. Later in the first period, Tyler got a breakaway and deked Negaunee's goalie to make the game 2-0. Ethan came out and took the next faceoff and took it down to Negaunee's zone and kept the puck in their zone for a minute. David finally got a shot off, which Negaunee's goalie saved, but Caleb was there for the rebound to make it 3-0.

We were pretty steady on our for checks and our back checking was a lot better. The second period was beginning and it seemed we had a nice handle on the game. We came out into the second period and really kicked it into overdrive. We were putting offensive pressure every shift and wound up scoring another 3 goals in the period. Tommy, Hanna and Ethan scored goals in the second. The Negaunee goalie was really doing a good job and kept them in the game.

It was the end of the second and the zamboni was coming out for a resurface. I really didn't know what to say because every aspect of our game was solid. I thought we could pass more and I needed to keep the kids at bay. I was thinking that overconfidence would be a really bad thing. Bob, Brian and I didn't say too much, we just told the kids to stay focused and work on our passing and winning races to the puck. The players were in a really good mood and it seemed they were level headed, which made my job easier.

The third period started and Negaunee came out firing. They were in our zone longer than they had been all day long. Matthew was making a few saves and making it look easy. A few minutes later, Hanna scored her second goal of the season on a very nice shot. I pulled back Caleb, Tyler, Ethan and CJ on defense to experiment to see if they could hold the blue line in our offensive zone and keep the puck out of our defensive zone. The players did an excellent job and Caleb wound up scoring from the blue line. We kept Negaunee out of the zone the final two minutes and the team had gotten their first shutout of the season winning 8-0.

The second game was the same as the first. We scored often and early. Negaunee's goalie had another solid game in net, but it wasn't enough. Ethan got his first hat trick. Two of the goals were shorthanded. We killed off 4 penalties and Nathan and Tyler had good scoring opportunities while we were shorthanded. It gave me an idea of trying a penalty kill using 3 forwards, called a diamond. It was something we could work on the following week in practice. We won the second game 9-0 and were now 4-0 on the season.

33

FIRST CHALLENGE

The following week we had played Iron Mountain, who was one of the toughest teams in the Upper Peninsula. I knew that we would have to have a top game to compete with them. I knew one of their players, Sawyer Perpich, who played defense, was as fast as I had seen at this age. All week long I tried to stay focused on team play, but the players were constantly talking about Sawyer and how good he was. I remember telling the players that they were skilled and they would have to give 110 percent to compete with them.

We took the ice on a late December Saturday morning. I greeted some of the player and parents I knew from Iron Mountain. I went into the locker room and reminded my players to loosen up and just play the game. They seemed uptight and didn't seem to be able to get relaxed. We took the ice and we actually had a nice warm up, Matthew looked sharp. The referee let the puck drop and off we went. The flow of the game was back and forth. We were evenly matched. About 5 minutes in, Sawyer broke free and got around CJ and came in hard at Matthew. Sawyer took a very nice shot and scored over Matthews's right shoulder.

This was the first time we were down this season. We played on through the first period at a stalemate. The second period came and the players were not nervous anymore. Tyler said to me, "We got this." With a funny smile on his face. About two minutes in, Ethan tripped a player on a breakaway and the referee gave Iron Mountain a penalty shot. This was a huge moment in the game. Mathew was set and the iron mountain player was coming. He made a nice shot, but Matthew stoned him. It was still 0-1. CJ was on the point the very next play and took a pass from Nathan and buried it past Iron Mountain's goalie. A few minutes later Iron mountain committed a tripping penalty. Brett took the puck from our zone and went coast to coast to score, making it 2-1 with a power play goal.

The second period ended and we felt the momentum. I knew that there was a lot of time for both teams. I Told Caleb to use his speed because he wasn't getting chances on the off wing. We went out in the third period and for the first 8 minutes there was a back and forth game. Both teams were having scoring opportunities. Ethan took the puck out of our zone and hit Caleb in full stride. Caleb took it down and scored, giving us the 3-1 lead. The next shift Tyler, came out and took it down, but hit the pipe. Our momentum was progressive and on the very next shift, Ethan did the same thing he did on his previous shift. He passed it to Caleb, streaking across the neutral zone that took it in and scored on his backhand. The game was now 4-1. It would stay at 4-1 even though in the final minute Iron Mountain attacked us with all they had.

Between games I had a chance to tell Sawyer that he looked really good and compliment the rest of their team. I felt our team climbed out of a hole and showed some intestinal fortitude. Bob was pleasantly surprised with our efforts. Bob at times can be a hard, but honest critic. Brian felt we looked good and had some really positive things going on. I talked to Sarah about her thoughts and she said Sawyer was tough and the defensemen had to play his speed honest. I told the players to take it easy and replenish fluids.

The second game was about to start and Matthew looked focused. The players were ready and out on the ice we went. The game started just like the last one. A stalemate of back and forth game. We were getting a lot more shots on goal, but their goalie was doing a solid job. Ethan finally scored with 6 minutes left in the first, assisted by Caleb and Tyler. We were up 1-0. Four minutes later CJ got a tripping penalty. Sawyer broke free and scored on a breakaway, ending the first period 1-1. This was our first time we didn't kill off a penalty this season.

The second period would define our team. We were playing hard and getting shots on goal, but their goalie was keeping us off the scoreboard. Iron Mountain came out and scored two goals putting us down 1-3.

With about 5 minutes left in the second, Tyler took one out of our zone and shelved on iron Mountain's goalie, making the score 2-3. I sent out Caleb on defense in the last minute. CJ did a D to D pass to Caleb. Caleb took it coast to coast with 15 seconds left and scored making the game 3-3. The next shift Tyler and Nathan would have one of the best passing combinations I would ever see, scoring with 1 second left, making the game 4-3 at the end of the second.

Momentum was on our side and we were starting to outshoot them 2-1. About 2 minutes into the third, Tyler scored with a great pass from Nathan, making the game 5-3. The game would be a steady see saw game but neither goalie would give up a goal and the final buzzer sounded. We won the game 5-3. It was a great way to start the season, but the coaches were happy with the outcome. We still had a lot of work to do.

The next day we were off to L'Anse to play Keweenaw Bay for a Sunday morning set of games. A two hour drive and then back home. I was curious on how they would play because some of their solid players had moved up to Bantams. We walked into the arena and I saw K-Bays players walking into the building. They were a little shorter, which obviously told me that they were very young. I went to our locker room where CJ had the music going and our players were getting ready.

We hit the ice and our warm up was crisp. Matthew looked ready to play and I had a good feeling he would have a good day. Tyler took the faceoff and brought it straight down for a quick shot on goal. We continued the offensive pressure with great passing. The players were communicating on the ice and shortly Nathan passed to Tyler who banged it home. A few minutes later Caleb scored on a nice wrist shot. 20 seconds later CJ scored. I felt a great flow of momentum in our favor. Tyler scored another goal towards the end of the first period making the game 4-0.

There were some opportunities to make some passes that weren't made. This didn't make me very happy or Bob and Brian either. I think some of our wings were frustrated because they were falling behind in the play. Even though we had a solid handle on the game I didn't want to lose our focus on developing skills and creating scoring opportunities. I was caught between a rock and a hard place. It was great that we had a big group of players who were developing into a solid two ways players, but we were dominating because of our age.

The second period, K-Bay made some adjustments and came out swinging, getting a few quick shots on Matthew that he stopped or were blocked by our defensemen. Our passing was getting better and the players were moving like we wanted. Ethan and Tyler scored the only goals of the second, but both goals were done by some very nice tick tack toe passing from Sydnee, Caleb, Hanna and Brett.

In between periods I asked Brian what he thought we should do since we were up 6-0. Brian responded that we should pull back and work on keeping the puck in their offensive zone. Tyler and Caleb led the way, paired with Ethan and CJ. We kept the puck almost the entire 3rd period, but we only squeaked out one goal by Sydnee. I was proud of our players for adjusting their rolls for the good of sportsmanship.

Our second year players were really developing quicker than I anticipated. Ethan, who moved up a year early, was really advancing in skill and ability. All of our players were developing and I refused to get away from some of our basic practice principals.

Our second game was almost exactly like the first. We came out hard and fast scoring 4 goals in the first and 4 in the second. Every goal was scored by a different player. Travis was fighting me a little and wanted to strictly play defense. I didn't fight him because I think playing forward made him uncomfortable. I was trying to find a way to sell it to him. I didn't have to sell it to Tommy who embraced the idea of playing some forward and show his skills. Tommy scored the last goal of the game and it ended 10-0.

We Left L'Anse with two victories, but most importantly, we left with some really nice team play. I knew I needed to find some small games to fine tune everyone's hockey skills and keep challenging them.

We had two weeks before our next games and we were missing because of the holidays. I needed this time to find a team that would show our weaknesses. I knew that some of the players were not challenged like I felt they should be. I started fine tuning practices with some individual work. I wanted Tyler and Caleb to face off more maybe to create some competitive practices that would rub off on our younger players. I sat at home writing matchups that would benefit every player on the team.

Matthew was a little bored and I think he was frustrated that he didn't see many shots, which was not a bad thing since our back checking and shot blocking was very solid. I asked Matthew what was going on. And He said that he felt his save percentage wasn't very good. I now saw what was going on. I think that his numbers in net were suffering from our great defense. When the opposition had a chance to score it was a great scoring chance. I just told him to keep focused and listen to what Tom told him. Matthew was your typical goalie and was starting to take the weight of the team on his shoulders. We were 8-0 and the kids were starting to talk about a perfect season.

I had a chance to corner Bob and ask him what we could do to get more competition. Bob said we should look to some of the AA or AAA programs. I agreed, but I couldn't find any teams that fit in our schedule. I prayed that this wouldn't haunt us in play downs. I looked for tournaments in Minnesota and Wisconsin. There were no tournaments that would fit into our schedule. I asked Sarah, who was our scheduler, to try and get Marquette or Houghton AA's to play us, but to no avail. I know that in the past Jim Young and I discussed that the players needed to be challenged by a better caliber team to improve. Of all seasons to try and test that theory this had to be the one.

This season had really given me the boost that I needed. I think when you lose your passion for something such as hockey, you need to find yourself and enjoy the game again. The parents were absolutely great to deal with and the players were even better. I felt revitalized and Sarah and I felt the players should get something special for Christmas from us again this year. We found it in our budget to get the players personalized jackets instead of getting each other gifts.

The practice before Christmas was a special one. I let the players do their shootout skills and scrimmaged at the end. While this was all going on, Sarah and Polly Clemens were setting up the pizzas and the jackets we bought for the team. The kids got off the ice and knew something was going on. They went into the locker room and got their equipment off, hurrying to get some of the pizza and pop that was waiting in the lobby for them. The players got some pizza and we handed out their jackets that Sarah had wrapped for them. The kids tore through the paper and put their jackets on with their eyes sparkling. The special feeling Sarah and I get from giving presents year after year was unforgettable each and every time.

Sarah and I went home with a really good feeling about what we had done and what the future would hold for all the kids. The holidays came and went. Our practices were getting more and more competitive with the constant assistance from our coaches. Dave Lundin was pushing our speed in our drills. Bob was constantly pushing the players by elevating his voice to increase the speed of the drills. Brian and I would get into the body contact and challenge the players at every opportunity. The practices were perfect and we ended each practice with a small game picked out by different players.

I was not only doing our practice but, our Bantams that were split between Ontonagon and us. I wanted to help as much as I could and didn't want to miss any practice. Jeff Baxter and I would take turns driving to Ontonagon every 4th week. Jeff and I had a candid conversation about the Bantams. I wasn't able to make many games for them, but I needed to so I could assist Dave Guilbault, Mike Morris and Adam with their advanced skills. Dave and Mike ran a really good practice and I knew I needed to participate with the kids to push them as well. I drove to Ontonagon and told Dave I was going to get more physical with our players to elevate their competition. Dave agreed. Mike would smile when I would check Drew, his son, getting him to keep his head up was crucial in his development. Justin Niemi was fast and I couldn't keep up to him anymore, so when I knew Justin would make a move I anticipated and gave him the body. Justin would smile and give it back.

Brady Guilbault had one of the hardest shots I have ever seen. I used Brady's shot with the blizzards AAA team to make some comebacks. I thought about a power play and how we could use Brady's shot, Justin's speed and Drew's hands to help us score. Jacob was working at my practices with Tom, which was helpful. I told Adam and Dave about a play that Eric Boyer taught me the previous summer. It took 20 minutes to get it. The play worked like a dream and all the Bantams were liking what they saw. Play downs were only a month away.

On the drive home, Jeff said he liked what he saw and thought we may have a chance to go downstate with both teams. For the first time I thought about the possibilities and how much fun that would be. Jacob mentored Matthew all season and I thanked him every opportunity. Jacob is a quiet kid who works his tail off each and every time he is on the ice. I would tell Jacob that his hard work would give him opportunities in the future that other goalies wouldn't get.

34

THE NEW YEAR

The New Year came and the day after, we had home games against K-Bay. I greeted the players and parents as they entered the Civic Center. I gave the kids one good pep talk before they hit the ice. K-Bay's goalie had been doing an incredible job against us. We had our warm up, did the national anthem and took the face off. K-bay had come out hard, but we countered with our speed. K-Bays goalie was keeping them in the first period, only letting in one goal, which was scored by Travis and assisted by Ethan and Caleb. Our defense was superb. K-bay didn't get a shot on goal in the first period.

The second period started and we came out much like the first, skating hard and making great passes. We were getting more scoring opportunities and it was showing by finally getting it by K-Bay's goalie. Tyler scored twice, Caleb, Sydnee, and Ethan each scored in the second period giving us a 6-0 lead at the end of the second period. We went into the locker room with the lead and a ton of momentum. Matthew made 5 saves that period, but we had been back checking big time.

Our passing was spot on and our shots were on. We came out into the third period a little overconfident. The first shift a K-Bay player took the puck past Ethan and split our defensemen and shot it past Matthew. The game was now 6-1. I kind of liked what was going on because it showed that they wouldn't quit. A few shifts later Ethan would score his second of the game, followed by his third. Brett scored with a nice assist from Ethan to make the game 9-1. Our team wouldn't allow another shot on

149

goal the rest of the game. K-Bays goalie did an excellent job making 48 saves on 57 shots.

The second game I wasn't going to move any players, no matter what the score. I wanted the players to adapt to the position they were in. I didn't want to be overconfident, but I did want them to keep working on their skills. I wanted our defense to get more shots on goal and our forwards to do more deflections, just like we had been practicing. It worked like a charm. We scored 4 first period goals and three in the second. All were from the point. We had been passing and rotating it towards the defense which gave us more scoring opportunities. Nathan scored on one of the best deflections of the day and Brett capped the game off with a sweet shot from the point that went over K-Bay's goalie's left shoulder. The game finished 9-0 and K-Bay's goalie had made 81 saves on 99 shots.

We had to go against Iron River on Sunday and I was anxious to see how we would do against them. They had skill and speed just like we did. Iron River was showing up to the rink and it seemed they were ready to play. We came onto the ice with a little nervousness I hadn't seen since we played Iron Mountain.

Tyler took the faceoff and took it right down for a quick shot on goal. We were getting shots on goal and Iron River would come back at us and get a shot on goal. Nathan got called for a rare penalty, which seemed to stop our momentum. Ethan and Tyler came out to kill off the penalty. I set up our diamond formation we had been working on, to see if we could create some offense. It worked perfectly. Tyler passed it to a streaking Ethan who deked the Iron River goalie giving us the 1-0 lead with a shorthanded goal. The next shift, CJ made a long pass to Caleb who shot it past Iron River's goalie to give us a 2-0 lead, both shorthanded. Caleb scored again about a minute later giving us the 3-0 lead. Tyler countered with his own goal with three minutes left in the first period. With two minutes left in the period Iron River committed a penalty and Tyler wasted no time scoring a power play goal on a breakaway with 20 seconds left giving us the 5-0 lead.

We started the second period a little slow for some unknown reason. We weren't playing like we were overconfident, but we were not winning the races to the puck. Each team exchanged shots on goal and the only goal was by Caleb on a breakaway half way through the period. The second period ended with without any fireworks. Both teams were playing very hard and it was almost like a tied game.

We went into the locker room for the 3rd period resurface. The players were in a really good mood and rightfully so. They had worked their tail off and it showed on the scoreboard. CJ wasn't too happy since he took two penalties, which we killed off with Nathan and David. I reminded the players that this game wasn't over and they were still fighting back.

We took the ice and right off the faceoff Iron River came at us harder than they had all game. After a quick shot off the post, Matthew made a fantastic back door save. It was no doubt that they had a plan to put the pressure in our zone. We fought them off with Matthew shining for the first time all year. I was very proud of him to answer back the pressure they were putting on him. The Third period ended with nobody scoring in the third and us winning 6-0.

I was very happy that the kids weren't getting overconfident. They were focused and using all the tools we could give them. The second game started and it was just like the beginning of the first game. It was deadlocked through the first five minutes, until Tommy scored with a nice pass from Caleb. Iron River answered right back and scored on the next play. About two minutes later Ethan scored on a deflection from CJ and Caleb. A minute later we were on the power play and Tyler stole the puck at center ice and brought it down for a power play goal. The first period ended 3-1 and a very tight game.

The second period started slow and there weren't many scoring opportunities. Iron River committed a tripping penalty and right away Tyler scored off Brett's shot from the point with an assist from Caleb for a power play goal. Two minutes later there was a hooking penalty committed by Iron River's goalie. We put a ton of pressure on Iron River's offensive zone and passed the puck beautifully. Caleb passed to Ethan who skated it around the circle then passed to CJ finding the back of the net, giving us a 5-1 lead. It was our 3rd power play goal of the game. We left the second period with the lead and a great deal of confidence.

Brian was very happy with our performance and thought we were winning the battles that we should. Joe Metzger was telling me that our passing was right on and to keep it up. I watched the resurface finish and told the players to do exactly what Joe said, "KEEP IT UP!" The third period started and Iron River put pressure on us immediately. Our defense was holding up and Matthew made some nice saves. We countered with pressure in Iron River's zone. Most of the period was back and forth until, with two minutes left, Caleb Johnson, for Iron River, scored on a really nice wrist shot. The game ended 5-2 and I thought we had played really solid in both games.

The following day we headed to Negaunee to play Ishpeming Concrete the other team from Negaunee we hadn't played yet. It was cold in the arena and the players were not their talkative selves. I wondered how I could fire them up and keep them focused. I gave the kids a story about how when I was playing at the squirt level, I played because I loved the game. I told them how every time I hit the ice, those were my fondest memories of my friends. I told them to bring that joy on the ice and play their hearts out. The players smiled and looked around the locker room. I felt that the little heart felt chat was heard loud and clear.

We hit the ice and started the game with great energy. Negaunee came out swinging. Negaunee put pressure on our zone and got a quick shot off. Matthew pushed it aside and Travis passed it to David to clear our zone. That would be the last shot they would have the entire period. Our offense was spot on, but we were missing the net. Half way through the period Sydnee scored from a Caleb assist. After a penalty committed by Negaunee we went on the power play and Nathan scored assisted by Tyler and Brett. A minute after that, CJ scored from the point with an assist from Tyler. With a minute left and controlling the period, Tyler broke away from Negaunee's defense and scored with 51 seconds left. We ended the period with a 4-0 lead.

In between periods, I told the players I was proud of them and that they needed to continue to pass the puck. The period started and Caleb scored about a minute in with an assist from Tyler. Negaunee started to fight back and clear the puck better than they had in the first period. This made our scoring opportunities fewer and fewer. Tommy and Brett made a couple of attempts to carry it up, but weren't successful. With six minutes left Tyler finally scored with an assist from Nathan. There wasn't any more scoring in the second period, leaving the score 6-0.

We went to the locker room with a lead and dominating the game. The players were winning most of their individual battles. Tyler and Caleb were moving back to defense and Brett and Tommy were moving up. I wanted to back off a little and work on getting the puck to the points to create deflection opportunities. It worked like a charm. A few minutes in Nathan scored on a Tyler shot from the point. David scored with a shot from Caleb who received a nice pass from Nathan. With only a few minutes left, Ethan scored on a pass from Tommy. The score was 9-0 and the players knew it was time to back off and pass the puck. The game ended and we were looking solid.

In-between games, the players were hanging around watching a midget game looking like a team should. They were all equal and they were acting like it. I always watch and see that the players are rehydrating and eating something. It was very nice to have a team who bought into nutrition and their play was showing it. The players were getting ready for the next game in the locker room and I heard the music banging from the outside. This made me very happy because our team continuity was solidifying.

We started the second and final game with much of the same as the first game. We dominated and controlled the puck. We scored 6 first period goals and never looked back. We scored three more in the second and backed way off and just played defense in the third period. The game ended with the exact same score 9-0 and it was our 8th shutout of the season. Most importantly, we were playing like a team. I was happy with our play and I knew with play downs the following week, which we needed to step it up even more.

35

PLAY DOWNS

The next practice Bob and I discussed getting the players to get more aggressive. It was already January 10 and half the season was over. Things were happening fast and I needed to contour our practices to have more speed and more competition. I worked on some drills to make this happen. I thought at the last minute to create some up-tempo man-on-man battles. Some of our younger players I needed to push a little harder. I thought they would benefit from this challenge. Monday and Wednesday practices were exactly that. Bob, Brian, Dave, Tom and I pushed the players and had a blast doing it. I think we were ready for Saturday's game with Iron Mountain.

We hit the ice and I called Tyler and Caleb over and told them that I wanted them to play to their level. Even though we had been playing really well, I thought they could play better and that would rub off on their teammates. I wanted to push the level of play regardless of who we were playing. The kids were listening when to back off of teams. All of our defensemen were playing well and Matthew was playing really solid when we needed him to. Our power play and penalty kill had been solid as well.

The game was about to start and the kids looked a little nervous. The puck dropped and the game was back and forth for the first few minutes. Iron Mountain broke the ice first with a breakaway goal from Sawyer Perpich. With two minutes left in the first period, Tyler broke free twice and scored on both occasions, giving us the 2-1 lead. Ethan then scored from a nice pass from Caleb with 54 seconds left. The first period ended with a 3-1 lead. The energy was great but Iron Mountain didn't give up.

The second period started with Sawyer, from Iron Mountain, scoring a goal 26 seconds in closing the lead to 3-2. Thirty seconds later Nathan scored from David, giving us the two goal lead again. The swing in momentum was back and forth the entire period. A minute later Iron Mountain scored again, gaining a bunch of confidence and making the game 4-3. Half way through the second period, Iron Mountain's Sawyer went on a breakaway and scored his third goal of the game making it 4-4. The second period ended at 4.

We went to the locker room and I told the players I wasn't pleased with our passing. I thought some of our skilled players thought they could do it on their own. I raised my voice and yelled a little to gain their undivided attention. Some players were not going as hard as they could and needed a wake-up call. After each coach gave their thoughts the players exited the locker room and went back to the ice.

We started the third with some energy. Tyler scored 43 seconds in with an assist from Caleb. A minute later Iron Mountain committed a penalty and Caleb scored with an assist from Ethan. The score was now 6-4 and I was hoping we could keep the momentum. Four minutes later Iron Mountain scored, keeping the game within reach at 6-5. After Matthew stopped Perpich on another breakaway we took the puck out of the zone and David passed it over to Tyler, who shot it in the back of the net. A Minute later Brett took the puck out of our zone and skated it and scored on a sweet shot giving us a 8-5 lead. Iron River countered, with two minutes left closing the lead to 8-6. With 5 seconds left Caleb scored with an assist from Brett and ending the game.

We shook hands with the Iron Mountain team. I thought they were very solid and never quit, which I like to see. Matthew made saves he needed to make to help us get by our first game of the play downs. We went back to the hotel before our next game to rest up. We were playing calumet next who was always tough. Sarah and I discussed our breakdowns and our successes. I deduced that our play had to be better if we were going to get out of the play downs and a chance to play at the district 8 UP finals.

We went back to L'Anse to play Calumet. They didn't have a large bench but the players were fast and skilled. We hit the ice and Brian told the players to have fun. It was a great piece of advice. The game started as fast as we had played all season long. The puck dropped and both teams were flying. I was proud of our players playing such a fast paced game. Calumet struck first with a nice goal 3:36 in. Tyler answered back 11 seconds later. Calumet then scored at 6:06, which Caleb countered with his own goal at 6:24. The first period ended with not many whistles and a ton of skating.

The second period started with a flurry of shots by our team. CJ scored 36 seconds in with and assist from Ethan. The game was dead locked for the next six minutes until Ethan broke free on a breakaway and deked the calumet goalie, making the game 4-2. Nathan scored just 8 seconds later with assists from Tyler and Ethan. Calumet then committed a penalty a few minutes later which allowed Nathan to score his second consecutive goal with an assist from Tyler, giving us the 6-2 lead on the power play. Calumet was far from done. They fought back and scored two goals in the final 3 minutes closing the gap to 6-4. Calumet had a definite momentum and Matthew made some saves towards the end of the period to keep it at 6-4. We went to the locker room a little stunned even though we had a two goal lead.

We had been getting burned on defense pretty steady. Their team speed was obvious and Bob and I discussed how our forwards needed to back check to assist our defensemen. I think the steady speed of the game was wearing on some of our players. I knew that the Calumet players had to be a little fatigued as well.

We went on the ice for the third period not knowing what was in store for us. Calumet came out firing on all pistons. They scored a minute in, closing the gap and gaining even more momentum. Three minutes afterward Calumet evened the game at 6 with a very good shot from the point. Tyler came on the ice and said something to Nathan before the faceoff. Tyler won the faceoff to Nathan, who passed it back and Tyler turned on the speed past Calumet's defense to score 14 seconds later. With two minutes left, Calumet got called for a checking from behind and we went on the power play. A few second in, Brett took a shot from the point which Nathan deflected, and scored the power play goal and his first hat trick of the season and giving us the 8-6 lead. Calumet came down 17 seconds later and scored on Matthew. Calumet called a time out. It gave me a chance to set up a last minute play. Caleb took the faceoff and passed it to Tyler who skated it down and took a shot on an empty net. Tyler missed the net and time ran out giving us the 8-7 win.

After the game, I was proud of the Calumet players and complimented the coach and players on their never give up attitude. It was one of the most energetic games I had been a part of. I talked to my players briefly in the locker room. I told them that I was proud of each and every one of them. Every player participated and made a difference. Sarah and I went back to the hotel kicked back and I started to look over everything that happened in both games. I thought that the players answered the challenge and I was proud of them. The kids were in the hall playing knee hockey with Brian and having a blast.

The Bantams were also playing in Baraga about 5 miles away. I got to see only one game. The Bantams had been struggling a little bit. Dave and Adam had been doing a good job with them all season long. Jacob was playing solid in net and the team had responded well.

It was Sunday and we had our last two games. The top 3 of 5 were going to the District finals. Iron River was our first opponent of the day followed by K-Bay. Our team preparation is always the same when it comes to Districts and play downs. I always make sure we have all the players get a good hearty breakfast. We then have a team warm up with some jumping, running, and stretching. I believe this helps not only our physical preparation but our mental preparation, as well.

We arrived at the rink with an nervous anxiety. Iron River was our first opponent of the day. We hit the ice with an excitement I hadn't seen all weekend. I called Tyler, CJ, and Caleb over to tell them it was time to do their usual pre game Captain duties. To go shake hands with the opposing coaches before we started the game. The boys did this before every game. Brian and Bob were getting the players pumped up while I talked to the three captains. I told them one thing, "Captains are team leaders, and you lead your team by example. This game will show your leadership. Take control of the game and have fun doing it." The glow in their eyes was unforgettable as well as the smile that came with it.

The puck dropped and it was like every other game we play against Iron River, back and forth. Iron River had three scoring opportunities in the first 3 minutes which Matthew made some very nice saves. Tommy started a breakout and passed it to Nathan who passed it to a streaking Tyler, who shelved it on Iron River's goalie. A minute later Iron River returned with a goal of their own. With only a few seconds left, Caleb made a nice pass to Tyler who was skating hard past the Iron River defense and scored right before the period ended. I was happy with our play overall, but I knew we could do better defensively.

The start of the second period showed the momentum we had gained was not leaving. Iron River committed a penalty shortly into the second period. We controlled the puck and Nathan passed it to Brett who was wide open at the point. Brett shot the puck and Tyler deflected it into the back of the net. Iron River was doing really well clearing the puck out of the zone, but we were not giving them any breathing room. Iron River committed another penalty for checking. We went on another power play. Ethan skated it up out of our zone and took a shot off Iron River's goalie which Tyler shot in the rebound for his fourth goal of the game. The period ended 4-1 and we were in control.

We went into the locker room with our team getting a ton of chances. Travis, Brett, CJ, and Tommy were playing outstanding defense. Matthew made some nice saves to help his defensemen out. Our forwards didn't seem to be slowing down. Hanna, Sydnee and David were quietly having a great game as well. There was nothing to tweak in-between periods, just to let them know the game wasn't over and keep giving 100 percent. The coaches didn't really say much. There was a quiet confidence amongst the players.

We started the third period with an energy that I was hoping they would bring. Iron River was playing us tough for the first few shifts but a penalty slowed their momentum. Thirty seconds in Tyler scored from a pass from Caleb with a very nice 2 on 1. It was Tyler's 5th goal and his 3rd power play goal of the game. A few minutes later Caleb scored on a pass from Ethan, making the game 6-1. With two minutes left I told the players they had to pass three times before shooting on net. Caleb scored again, with assists from Tyler and Ethan. The game came to an end at 7-1 final. We had advanced to the Districts with that win.

We went to Baraga to see how the Bantams were doing. When we walked in I was surprised to see that we were down to K-Bay. The Bantams were up and down all season long. It seemed they could fire on all pistons two consecutive games. They were losing going into the third when Brady Guilbault lit the lamp twice on back to back shifts to bring it within one. With a minute left Drew Morris had a nice pass to Justin Niemi who shelved it on K-Bay's goalie tying the game. The game ended. Tied and the Bantams were going on to the districts. I thought it was a very gritty game that they deserved. We then headed back to L'Anse.

The second and last game of the play downs was against K-Bay. The players were ready and I think they wanted to get on the ice and finish the weekend. Ethan took the faceoff and won it to Caleb who passed it back to Ethan, who split the defense and scored 9 seconds in. Two minutes in, Caleb scored on a nice pass from Ethan. Ten seconds later Tyler received a pass from Tommy and scored our 3rd goal in three minutes. A few minutes later Hanna scored off some nice passes from Nathan and Ethan. I told the players that I was going to change up the lines after the first. The players were looking good and I was proud of them. Caleb then scored a goal off a rebound shot from Ethan, making the game 5-0 half way through the first. With two minutes left, Nathan scored off a Tommy shot. A minute later Sydnee scored off passes from Nathan and Tyler.

The first period finally came to an end. It was 7-0 and I needed to change up lines. The rest of the game I had the defensemen playing up on forward hoping to slow down our offensive outburst. I told the players that they couldn't shoot until we had completed 3 passes. The only goal we scored in the second was Tommy from CJ and David. The game was flying by because of run time. The third period was much of the same except I told the players 5 passes before they could shoot. K-Bay didn't get many scoring opportunities in the third. We scored two more goals in the third by CJ and Caleb. The game came to an end at 10-0. We shook hands, with K-Bay and went home.

At the next practice I told the players what my thoughts were of the play downs. I told them I was happy with their overall play. I thought our team bounced back and we never quit. I then informed them that we needed to keep up that level of play no matter who we were playing. Brian worked the players in some drills he wanted to run, which gave me a chance to talk to the captain's one at a time and tell them how proud I was of them.

January 22, we had to go to Iron Mountain for a couple of games. We arrived in Iron Mountain not knowing what to expect. We didn't have Hanna, who was at a basketball game back home and Travis was sick for the first game. We hit the ice and the players looked really focused. The puck dropped and three minutes in Nathan scored with assists from

Tyler and CJ. The game was back and forth for a while until Ethan took a hooking penalty, putting us shorthanded. This gave us an opportunity to try the diamond we had been working on in practice. A minute in Caleb intercepted a pass and took it on a breakaway. Caleb deked the goalie and scored a shorthanded goal. The first period ended and we had a good deal of momentum with a 2-0 lead.

The second period started with much of the same back and forth stalemate. About 4 minutes in Tyler scored on a wrist shot assisted by David and Brett. Not even a minute later Iron Mountain passed it around and scored on Matthew, making the game 3-1. Forty five seconds later Caleb skated the puck down and passed it to Sydnee who passed it to Nathan, who passed it back to Caleb for a one timer. We had done a really good job of passing thus far. The period ended with a 4-1 lead.

Bob told the players that we needed to pass a little harder since Iron Mountain was picking some of the passes off. Brian went over our diamond penalty kill with the players. We left the players alone to listen to the music until the resurface was finished.

We hit the ice in the third period with Tyler taking the faceoff. This lead gave me a chance to tinker with some lines. I put Nathan and Ethan together for a change and Tyler and Caleb together. Two minutes in Tyler scored with assists from Sydnee and Caleb. Twenty seconds later Nathan scored on a nice pass from Ethan. The next play, Caleb got called on a tripping penalty. We went out to work on our diamond again. It only took ten seconds and Ethan took a breakaway pass from Nathan. Ethan took it down and shot it into the netting behind Iron Mountain's goalie. After killing off another penalty, the period was dead locked. Then Ethan scored making the game 8-1. The game had ended and I was surprised we played so well without two of our players.

The next game Travis said he was feeling better and wanted to play. The team got a quick bite in-between games and went to the locker room to listen to some music before the game. The kids loved the hard rock before the game. It really pumped the players up. We hit the ice ready to play. The puck dropped and Iron Mountain was hustling and winning most of the battles in the beginning. Four minutes in Brett scored with assists from David and CJ. About 43 seconds later CJ scored from the point on a pass from Ethan, giving us the 2-0 lead. Three minutes later

Brett took a shot from the point and it was redirected by Tyler. The period ended 3-0, which was pretty good since we had to kill off two penalties.

The second period Iron Mountain really tightened up their defense. Most of the second period was back and forth with the exception of one break away that Caleb scored on. We went into the third period with confidence and pride. After a short resurface we hit the ice again. The period was deadlocked until Nathan scored off a Tyler pass, giving us the 5-0 lead. Two minutes later David scored on a rebound shot from Caleb. The period was going by fast and we got a little lax and Iron Mountain scored with 40 seconds left. We won the game 6-1 and we were an amazing 20-0 on the season.

On Sunday we prepared to play Ashland for two games at home. Brian and Bob did most of the talking before the first game. I knew we had a really solid team with coachable kids, but what I didn't know was how they would respond to different coaching styles. I wanted Bob and Brian to talk to the players for both games. I would sit and give my support.

We went on the ice and did our normal warm up. The players for the first time were a little overconfident. I wasn't sure why this was happening but I was intrigued what the results would be. Ashland came out hard and played with a lot of passion. David finally broke the ice 6 minutes in with an assist from Tyler. Thirty seconds later Tyler scored on a breakaway. A minute after that, David scored his second goal of the game with assists from Tyler and Nathan. Forty seconds later Tyler scored off a CJ shot from the point. We had a good lead, but we were not passing like I thought we should be. The period ended 4-0.

The second period Ashland really came out and played solid, but our defense was keeping shots away from Matthew. We only allowed 1 shot in the second. There was only one goal scored in the second. Caleb scored off a rebound from Ethan's shot. It was getting more and more evident that our passing was dwindling. We went into the locker room with a 5-0 lead but it didn't feel like it.

Bob told the players that they were not playing that well. Brian explained that without passing they were not going to keep improving. I agreed with both coaches and added that we needed to keep focused. We hit the ice after the resurface. We came out firing and started passing like I knew we could. Two minutes in Ethan scored off passes from David and Brett. A minute later Tyler scored with passes from Nathan and CJ. We were starting to look like the team I knew we could be. Thirty seconds after that Tyler scored again with an assist from Nathan who got a playmaker for 3 assists. The rest of the period we passed, but didn't score. The first game ended 8-0 and we didn't look like I wanted us to.

Sarah and I were talking between games trying to figure out what was going on. Sarah suggested that there was too much worry about who was getting hat tricks and not about playing the game. I was going to look at the next game and figure out what was going on.

We hit the ice with a cocky attitude. I think we were a little too overconfident. Ashland came out swinging like it was a championship fight. Ashland only had 5 shots on goal the entire first game, this time they had 8 in the first period. Ashland struck first on a nice shot giving them the 0-1 lead. Eight seconds later Tyler took it down the ice off the faceoff and scored from the hash marks. The first period ended in a tie and our players had a down look on their face.

The coaches rallied the players together and told them one thing, "Play hard." There wasn't anything else to say I think they knew they were taking the game for granted. Back on the ice, Ethan took the faceoff and you could tell the players were now focused. In the first couple of shifts we were locked up and Ashland had some scoring opportunities that Matthew stopped. With five minutes in Ethan scored on a pass from Caleb, giving us our first lead of the game. A minute later Tyler got a breakaway and shot it in the upper left corner. Tyler again scored a few minutes later with an assist from David. The second period ended and we were up 4-1.

I walked into the locker room and I got the feeling that the players thought they won the game already. I was very perturbed by this. I told the players as I had been telling them at almost every practice, "You need to give the effort and quit trying to think you are." Bob, Brian and I were impressed with Ashland's no quit attitude. I knew they weren't going to give up. I still had a feeling that something wasn't right. The resurface was over and we hit the ice for the third period.

The kids were skating around like they didn't care. I wasn't sure if they were bored or if they thought they were that good that they didn't have to work. Ashland looked focused and they proved it. Sydnee scored about three minutes in off a rebound that Caleb had shot. Ashland refused to pack it in. Ashland scored back to back goals making the game 5-3 with 7 minutes left to play. It was a back and forth game until Tyler scored with 2:27 left in the game. Ashland refused to give in and came right back, scoring a goal 14 seconds later. The game was really interesting now. I called a time out to talk to the players. I told them one thing, "Win the races to the puck." That was it. After the time out Caleb got control and brought it into Ashland's zone. We passed the puck around and didn't leave their zone. The game ended 6-4. I was happy to see Ashland didn't quit but I wasn't happy to see that our team was overconfident right before districts.

It was fortunate that we had Negaunee coming to town the next day. I wanted to let the kids play without pressure. Brian and I were thinking about just letting the kids be kids. We had a tournament in Iron Mountain the following week and I wanted to have the kids relax and enjoy their season. I was more nervous about the pressures the kids instilled in themselves. I figured the more we kept lines the same the more comfortable they would feel.

On Sunday January 30 we played Negaunee. The kids were in a good mood and we didn't want to ruin any of our player's confidence by mentioning our last game. We won the first game 13-1 with some fantastic passing and some great team effort. The great thing about this team is that they have an awesome work ethic and an ability to excel from adversity. Every team I have ever coached had good communication, but this team by far was the best. The second game was much of the same, winning 9-1.

Sarah and I drove home as I thought about the pressure of not losing a game the entire season could be mounting up. I knew we had to lose because no one goes undefeated. I was fearful that the one loss could end this incredible season. When we got home Sarah started calling more AA and AAA programs to play. Nobody was available to play. I started to look on the computer later that night and I noticed that some of the players and parents were getting in the hoopla of who was scoring and we were undefeated. This began to worry me. I felt like this could be a distraction and destroy this great season the kids were having. I emailed the parents and set a mandatory parents meeting during our next practice.

On Monday we had our parents meeting. I told the parents I wanted to address some potential problems. First thing was, "Don't worry about who is and isn't scoring. The kids don't care if you don't." The second was parents were talking on the internet about being undefeated, and I asked them to stop. I told the parents to be proud of what their player is doing and enjoy the ride. The parents as a whole knew what I was telling them was true and they honored my wishes. I didn't want to think about records or winning because I thought it would take away from this season.

It was unbelievable that I didn't get any resistance from the parents. I felt they knew what was at stake. The players were having fun and there wasn't any petty squabbling amongst them. There was excellent practice after excellent practice. Our preparation was spot on, and the teams we played all played their hearts out. With only two weeks till districts this tournaments timing couldn't be any better.

36

IRON MOUNTAIN TOURNAMENT

On February 4 we arrived in Iron Mountain to play a very tough Calumet Mohawk Legion team. We hit the ice late on a Friday night. Our team looked ready to play and I think we were a little intimidated by their size and speed. Calumet scored first, three minutes in. Their passing was very good and they really hustled after the puck. The rest of the period was dead locked until Tyler scored on a Caleb breakout pass with a minute left in the period. Calumet was playing excellent and it was an exciting game.

The second period started and again it was deadlocked the first 6 minutes of the period. Tyler finally broke the tie with a goal assisted from Nathan and David. A minute later Ethan shot it high past Calumet's goalie with an assist from Caleb. The game was now 3-1 and we were making the best of our scoring opportunities. Calumet refused to fold, scoring on a great shot, pulling the game within one. A minute and a half later David responded with a goal of his own with assists from Tyler and Nathan. The period would end 4-2 and we went to the locker room for a resurface.

Bob thought we were playing awesome and he told the kids how proud he was of them. Brian told the kids to work hard because we were on the power play to start the third period. I really didn't say anything. I asked Matthew how things were going in front of the net and he responded, "Ok but we can do better." Both teams were getting a ton of shots and I figured sooner or later one team would explode.

We started the third period with our power play line. Forty eight seconds in Ethan scored with assists from Nathan and Tyler. It wasn't 30 seconds later that Nathan got on a breakaway and put it past Calumet's goalie, making the game 6-2. Calumet responded like they did all game, scoring from some nice passing cutting the lead to 6-3. Calumet then committed a tripping penalty taking Tyler down, who would have had a breakaway. A minute and a half in Nathan scored again with an assist from Caleb. Twenty seconds later Nathan scored again, giving him a hat trick and a playmaker in the same game. Again Calumet refused to give up and came down the ice and scored, making the score 8-4. There were only 4 minutes left and our strong legs started to show. Ethan scored two goals in 23 seconds assisted from Brett and Caleb. The game ended 10-4. I believe it was our best game all season long.

We went back to the hotel room to relax and do some pondering about the great game we had played. The players were having a really good time playing knee hockey in the hallway. Bob was pleased with the kid's performance. I always try to get some parents views as well as the other coaches about every game we play. I use this in my logs to help make decisions if I am stuck between ideas.

After a good night rest we headed back to the rink to play the other Iron Mountain team, Binks, who were undefeated in the other CUP league division. We hit the ice and our players looked really sharp and excited to play. The game started and it looked like we were in for a hard fought battle. Three minutes in Caleb scored on a breakaway assisted by Ethan and CJ. Eight seconds later Caleb took the puck from an Iron Mountain defensemen, deking the goalie and making it a quick 2-0 start with a shorthanded goal. The next shift Nathan scored off a Tyler shot and a Brett pass. We were 4 minutes in and we were looking really good. The rest of the period both defenses were solid not letting in many shots. With 17 seconds left in the first, Sydnee scored off Tyler's rebound, assisted by Tommy. The first period ended with us having a 4-0 lead.

The second period, Binks came out and put a quick one on the board a minute in and another a minute later, to cut the lead in half. Tyler responded 45 seconds later on a breakaway, making the game 5-2. Sydnee then scored her second goal of the game off a pass from Caleb and Ethan. The game was going back and forth when Binks lit the lamp again off a breakaway making the game 6-3. Caleb scored his third of the game, assisted by Ethan. Towards the end of the second, Ethan redirected Brett's shot from the point extending our lead to 8-3. Tyler scored at the end of the second with an assist from Nathan to end the second period 9-3.

We went into the locker room not only with the lead, but a big boost of confidence. The players were jamming to the music playing and we let them enjoy the moment. After the resurface we left the locker room more confident and happier than I had seen them all season. We hit the ice and I knew we had to play some tough defense, because Binks would not give up. Binks came out and scored a minute and a half in on a breakaway. Our defense was starting to play it safe and refused anymore breakaways. With 10 minutes left Caleb scored his 4th goal of the game with an assist from Ethan. With one minute left, we went on the power play and I instructed Tyler to get the puck and waste some time. Tyler shot the puck in from center ice and after a bad bounce, the puck went past Binks goalie, ending the game 11-4.

I was astounded that we were playing better and better. The parents were very pleased and were enjoying the moment. Sarah and I went out to eat, and then headed back to the rink to play the other Iron mountain team.

Before the game I was talking with Sawyer's, from Iron Mountain, dad about how impressed I was with his son's development. I really liked a lot of the players that were on the Northern Michigan Chill AAA summer team. All the kids were good players and very well behaved.

We finally hit the ice later that Saturday night against the other Iron Mountain team and I knew that this game would be very difficult. Ethan took the faceoff and two minutes later he scored on a pass from Caleb. The next shift Tyler broke free and scored on a nice shot in the upper corner. The very next faceoff, Tyler won. Nathan passed it to Tyler who scored again on the same shift. Iron Mountain called a time out. The momentum that we had was suddenly gone as Iron Mountain's defense, Sawyer in particular, was as solid as I had ever seen him. Our shots the rest of the period didn't get the opportunities we were getting earlier. The period ended 3-0.

The second period showed some awesome defense on both sides. CJ, Brett, Tommy and Travis were having their best game defensively, all season long. Our forwards were back-checking, making it difficult for Iron Mountain to make passes. Iron Mountain was solid. Nathan scored the only goal of the period, assisted by Hanna and Tyler. We left the ice with a 4-0 lead and a resurface.

We went to the locker room very quietly. I think the players thought that they hadn't been playing well. That was far from the truth. Our forwards and defensemen were doing what they had been working on all season long. We returned to the ice after a short resurface. Iron Mountain came out trying to get the puck deep, but Tommy and Brett were quick to clear the zone. CJ and Travis were hustling and making great break out passes. The puck left our zone just as fast as it entered. Three minutes in, Iron Mountain committed a penalty and put us on the power play. Tyler wasted no time shooting it past their goalie, assisted by Nathan. The game would stay that way all the way till the end. With 30 seconds left Sawyer got past Travis and was headed on a breakaway. Ethan and Caleb were closing in but were too far back. Sawyer, from Iron Mountain, took the shot and Matthew saved it. The game had ended 5-0 and it was our team's incredible 11th shutout of the season.

Sarah and I returned to the hotel. We took back some food and hung out with the parents for an hour. I then went to bed to rest up for our next game with Iron River. Adam called me as I was getting into bed. The Bantams were doing ok, but needed to win in the morning if they would have a chance to play for the UP championship. I told Adam I would call them before the first game.

The next morning I woke up and called Adam, who put me on speaker phone. I told the players, "Play your heart out and I will be at the next game. Refuse to lose." I then told them I was proud of them, but their work wasn't finished. I then walked upstairs and got my bag to go to the rink. Sarah was more excited about going to Marquette to see the Bantams than us winning this tournament.

We went to the rink and the players were quiet for some unknown reason. They weren't talkative. I was thinking it was because they were nervous. We hit the ice and we were not very crisp and didn't look very fast in our warm ups. Brian was trying to fire them up but they were still pretty quiet. Bob figured they were tired from 3 tough games this weekend. The puck dropped a minute and a half in Caleb scored, assisted by Ethan. The rest of the period was a typical Ironwood versus Iron River game deadlocked.

The second period the players were starting to look a little livelier. Ethan went out and scored on the very first shift. The rest of the period

Ethan was on fire, scoring 3 more goals, giving him 4 for the game. The defense was getting shots and the forwards were feeding them. CJ, Tommy, Brett and Caleb all had assists on Ethan's goals. The 2nd period ended with us having a 5-0 lead and Matthew was focused and playing solid. The Third was a stalemate, there was only one goal scored and Caleb scored it assisted by Ethan. Ethan had points on all of our goals. The game ended 6-0 and this weekend could have been our most important because each of our players had gained confidence.

After a quick group of pictures with the championship trophy it was time to hustle to Marquette. The Bantams had won and they were playing a very talented Negaunee team for the Bantam B UP championship and the right to represent district 8 in Livonia, Michigan. Sarah and I got to the rink ahead of Polly Clemens and Jeff Baxter. Each of us was trying to get to Marquette as fast as we could.

I walked into the arena and straight to the locker room. Brady was the first I saw with a big grin on his face. I gave a few high fives to the players and walked out to talk to Adam. The kids had really been playing well, and as fate would have it, here we were. I couldn't get out of my mind that we had the chance to play for a state championship with two teams. It was surreal, but this is when hard work pays off.

We started the game and Jacob was making some awesome stops. Negaunee's goalie was countering with some great saves of his own. Negaunee capitalized twice in the first to give them the lead. The second was deadlocked but we fell behind 4-2. In-between periods we were shorthanded and Dave Guilbault gave a very good speech that motivated the players. Eugene Soumis and I were discussing how we could change our luck. I told Brady that he had to make it happen. I explained the diamond formation. Drew, Tony and Justin were going to have to be fast and exact on their passes. Jacob was going to have to play better than he ever had to get past Negaunee.

We hit the ice down by 2. Right off the face off Negaunee came down and right after us. Drew got the puck and lifted it past Negaunee's defense to Brady. Brady took it in and put it past Negaunee's goalie. The next shift Jonny got the puck and made a perfect pass to Brady who took a monster slap shot and beat Negaunee's goalie to tie the game at 4. Two shorthanded goals caused their coach to call a time out. Dave and Adam were praising the players. You could feel the momentum change. We were finally on full strength and Tony skated the puck down and gave us the lead with another slap shot. Negaunee wouldn't quit. They came after us shift after shift but Jacob was on and wasn't letting anything by. I can still hear the echoes of the rink, as the clock ticked down, 3-2-1 then the screaming. We were going to Livonia to play for the State Finals!

We took pictures and headed home. I was very proud of the Bantams and now it was time to prepare for the Squirts. I knew it wasn't going to be easy, but I was confident that we wouldn't quit and we would work hard. After getting home I started to get practice plans ready, as I had only two weeks to get the players ready to play one of the most exciting times of the year, UP District Finals.

37

DISTRICTS

That following Monday at practice I think I skated the squirts as hard as I have ever skated any team. The team needed an early work out that would help refocus our desires and keep our work ethic intact. The retention training we gave them would help them for the long haul. The edge work would keep the focus on skating. In between each and every hard drill we would slow it down with simple drills like passing and shooting. We focused hard and the players responded with hard work. Everything was going according to plan. I knew if we were to slip up at any point it would be my fault and mine alone. The kids were proven winners.

On Friday February 18, 2011, we arrived in Hancock, Michigan to play at Houghton County Arena. Our first game was against Marquette. Marquette has a long history of excellent hockey. Before the game I wanted to make sure that every player knew that this weekend was meant for fun. They were here because they earned it. "Continue to work hard and good things will happen no matter if you win or lose." I said.

We hit the ice and Tyler's line started like we did most games. We came out firing. Great passes with unbelievable hustle. Caleb scored on a breakaway 2 minutes in. A few minutes after that Nathan continued to play solid hockey by scoring a garbage goal off Tyler's shot. A minute later Caleb scored his second goal off a deflection from Ethan and Tommy. Marquette's goalie, Tyler Bergwall, was unbelievable in net. He made a ton of great saves and was helping keep Marquette in the game. The first period ended 3-0.

171

You could tell the players had prepared for this weekend and this game, by the way they were playing. The second period we came alive, winning individual battles for the puck. Tyler scored on a nice give and go from Nathan. Marquette answered back scoring on a shot from the point. Later in the second, Nathan scored off a give and go from Tyler. The swing of momentum was happening in our favor. Ethan then scored a minute later on a breakaway. With only a minute left Sydnee scored on a rebound that Ethan shot from a Caleb pass. We had a 7-1 lead at the end of the second.

The players wanted to jam and listen to music. The coaches didn't have much to say. The players said it all with their hustle. After the resurface we hit the ice. I was happy with the total effort by every player. Marquette came out pumped and was doing some really nice passing. After a few minutes Marquette scored on a nice back door pass. Matthew didn't see the Marquette player on the back side. A minute later a Marquette player received a penalty. We set up our diamond and immediately Tyler threw a pass past Marquette's defenseman and Ethan took it down and shot it in the net. The rest of the game was back and forth and the game ended 8-2, in our favor.

I was happy with the way we started the weekend. It was now back to the hotel to relax for two games on Saturday. The parents set up a great potluck and the players were having a great time. Afterwards, the players were played some knee hockey or just relaxed in their rooms. Sarah was hanging out with Polly. I just wanted to think and keep preparing for each game.

Saturday February 19 we went to Houghton County Arena to face off against Negaunee's Ok Industrial. We had played them two times already this season with some success, but in Districts, some teams really play their best. We hit the ice and had a really good warm up. The puck dropped and we had immediate pressure on Negaunee's offensive zone. Negaunee came down the ice two minutes in and put the puck in the net, giving them a quick 1-0. After a few minutes of back and forth hockey, Negaunee had a nice break out. Tyler picked the puck off and put it in the net. Two minutes later Caleb shot it high and scored from outside the faceoff circle. The game was now 2-1. We had momentum and it didn't stop. Caleb came up the ice with Ethan and was passing it back and forth when Caleb shot it in the net for his second goal of the game.

Negaunee's coach was screaming at his players uncontrollably. I noticed this and I thought of a plan to get him to stop yelling at his coaches and the referees. Tyler committed a tripping penalty so we set up our diamond. It took about 30 seconds and Caleb fed a pass to Ethan who took it down the ice and deked the goalie to make it 4-1 with a shorthanded goal. Negaunee's coach came unglued. Yelling and clearly upset. I then called a time out. I said to the kids," You hear that, It is quiet in here except for one guy yelling. Good Job Keep it up." I think it helped Negaunee because they came back and had some scoring opportunities.

The second period, Negaunee's players really brought out their best performance I had seen thus far. Caleb scored about 5 minutes into the period with an assist from CJ. A few minutes later Negaunee refused to give up, scoring on a nice breakaway making the game 5-2. The second period would end with both teams not being able to score.

The third period started and I noticed Negaunee's players had a little pep in their step. 30 seconds in, Negaunee had some very nice passing and buried it behind Matthew. A minute later Sydnee scored off a rebound that Tyler shot, making the game 6-3. Two minutes later one of Negaunee's players stole the puck in our zone and shot it in the net, pulling the game to 6-4. Two minutes later Negaunee committed a penalty and put us on the power play. I knew this was huge because we were having a difficult time with Negaunee. About a minute in Tyler scored off some nice passing from Ethan and Caleb, making the game 7-4 with four minutes left. The last minute Negaunee pulled their goalie and really came out scoring with 20 seconds left. We killed off the last 20 seconds and left with a 7-5 victory.

In the locker room I told the kids, "At Districts you can never underestimate an opponent. You have to bring your best effort each and every game. Get some rest, rehydrate and get ready to play Iron River." I left the locker room with a nervous feeling. We hadn't played too well, but they didn't quit either. Sarah gave me her opinion about the game, which wasn't favorable, but it was out of our control.

We arrived at Dee Stadium in Houghton for a 6:00 pm game. For some reason I knew that Iron River was coming for blood. I knew they not only needed this game, but they wanted it bad, since some people were starting to talk about who would be the first to ruin our undefeated season.

We went on the ice and had a very mediocre warm up. I thought we looked flat. Bob and Brian were trying to motivate the kids, but nothing was working. I was thinking as the referee dropped the puck, that maybe the nerves were too much and the pressure was starting to show in our play. The first period was awesome by both teams. Not many shots, but a lot of pass attempts and great defense. Caleb Johnson from Iron River had a breakaway and scored with 44 seconds left. The period ended 1-0.

In between periods I told the players, "There is no score. It is always 0-0. Play your heart out and leave this rink a winner no matter what the score." The players looked around and went to the net with Matthew for a little pep talk of their own. It was here where the captains and Matthew took control of their team. They got what we were trying to install in them. I think they felt in that moment, they knew this was their time, their team.

The second period we looked like we did earlier in the season. Half way through the second an Iron River player committed a penalty. Twenty seconds later Tyler took an Ethan pass and buried it past Iron River's goalie, tying the game 1-1. With a minute left Brett carried the puck up and gave a great pass to Caleb, who shot it high glove side. The second period ended with a 2-1 lead.

We went to the locker room with the lead and some momentum. I told the players, "Do your best. That's all I could ask for. It isn't about winning or losing, it's about being a team." Brian and Bob kept with the positive vibe we were giving the players. The zamboni came off the ice and we walked out to the stadium door ready to play.

The third started out with Iron River catching us off our guard and putting a lot of pressure on our offensive zone. Iron River tied it up on some nice passing. It was back and forth for 5 minutes. Tyler took the puck up on the right side of the rink and all 5 Iron River players followed him into the corner. Tyler pushed the puck up the boards where CJ took the puck and buried a hard wrist shot high past Iron River's goalie. Iron River came back, but our defense tightened up. Tommy got called for a tripping penalty. Nathan and David kept the puck in Iron River's zone the entire two minutes. The last minute Iron River had a chance to score, but Travis and CJ were excellent in front of Matthew. Matthew made a save with a second on the clock and we sealed the victory.

I got to the hotel and found out that Houghton, Marquette, Iron Mountain and us had all made it to the semifinals. I told the players to have an early night, eat, and hydrate. The players listened like they had all season. The players looked relieved and weren't nervous at all. Brian, Bob and myself were nervous and for obvious reasons.

In the morning we had a team breakfast along with a little run, followed by some team stretching. The players looked ready. We were playing home town Houghton in the semifinals and the right to play for the District Championship. We had played our best hockey in the morning and this was a 9:00 am game. The kids were jamming to some hard rock before the game. They seemed mentally prepared. The only thing I told them was, "Have fun. Play your heart out." The players darn near ran out of the locker room to get on the ice. I stopped Matthew and had a quick word with him. I told him, "Chewy, that was his nickname, what gets a team the Stanley cup?" Chewy responded, "A hot goalie." I smiled and told him, "Be that goalie."

The period started deadlocked. The teams both had speed and skill. Our defense was playing outstanding and owning the blue line. Houghton only had one shot in the first period and it was on a breakaway that Chewy stopped. With a minute and a half left Caleb broke free from Houghton's defense and deked the goalie with a sweet backhand, giving us the 1-0 lead. The next shift Tyler broke free and scored on a hard shot in the slot. We ended the first period 2-0.

There was a huge amount of speed on Houghton's team. I was concerned, but I was confident in our defense and our back checking. Our passing was getting more confident. 2 minutes in Caleb scored on passes from Ethan and Sydnee. A minute and half later Caleb scored his third of the game with an assist from Ethan. A minute after, that Tyler shelved one past Houghton's goalie with an assist from Caleb. Houghton was playing excellent, but we were making the most of our scoring opportunities. With 5 minutes left in the second, Ethan got a breakout pass from Caleb and deked the goalie, making it 6-0. The second period was dead locked and Chewy had made some very nice saves to keep Houghton off the scoreboard.

The third period was a grueling stalemate. Neither team was getting any scoring opportunities. Towards the end of the period, Houghton was attempting to get it past our defense but Brett, Tommy, Travis and CJ were prepared and cleared the zone quickly. Houghton pulled their goalie and Tyler scored off a nice pass from Nathan. We ended the game 7-0, with a nice team effort.

We went back to the hotel and then Sarah and I went out for a bite with Polly and Matthew. This gave me a great chance to talk to Matthew at length about hockey in general. We had some good food and some good laughs, and then we headed back to the hotel for the long wait before the game. The kids were watching some hockey movies before the game. Marquette beat Iron Mountain to earn the right to play us in the championship.

It was time we headed to Dee Stadium. I was nervous, but confident in our team. The kids were jamming to some heavy metal before the game and the coaches left the players alone. Right before it was time to go out Tyler asked if we could go to the stadium door because the locker room was hot. As we sat waiting for the referee's to go on the ice I noticed the players were not too nervous, but anxious to get going. We went on the ice and had a great warm up. Marquette worried me a little because they had some very nice skill and their goaltending was solid.

The game started fast up and down the ice. About 3 minutes in Marquette struck first. It was a nice goal that made its way past Chewy. It was a minute later and Ethan broke loose and shot it past Tyler Bergwall. The game was tied and remained that way thanks to nice goaltending both ways.

The second started with our passing spot on. Nathan scored a minute and a half in with an assist from Tyler. It was dead locked for another few minutes until Caleb stole the puck from a Marquette defensemen and scored. Then Tommy got called for a trip and we were shorthanded with 4 minutes left in the second. I knew this was a very important part of the game. Nathan and David were some of our best penalty killers. Both players didn't disappoint, they showed great effort killing the whole penalty and even getting a scoring opportunity. With 31 seconds left Tommy made a breakout pass to Hanna who made a nice pass to Tyler, who scored on a breakaway. The second ended with us having a 4-1 lead.

We went to the locker room with a great deal of confidence. Brian and Bob told the players to keep the pressure up and I gladly supported them. I went into the hallway and talked to Sarah about what she saw. After years of watching me coach and the kids play, her opinion mattered to me. She said she saw a whole team effort that every player was contributing. She was happy with not only our defensive coverage but our offensive as well. We discussed how Marquette's goalie, Tyler Bergwall, was keeping them in the game.

We took the team back out on the ice and the players went to the net with Chewy for a quick motivational speech. I am not sure what was said but I know CJ and Chewy were doing some yelling. The puck dropped and Marquette came out hard and fast, as I thought they would. Tyler, Nathan and Hanna were back checking to help get the puck out of our zone. The next shift, CJ passed it out of the zone to Ethan who passed it to Caleb, who beat the defense and buried the puck. The game was going back and forth until Tyler took a nice pass from Brett and shot it "Where MA MA hides the cookies." The game was now 6-1 with three minutes left. We killed off the time and the parents were yelling the count down, 7-6-5-4-3-2-1, then a triumphant scream, "YES."

The players were all jumping on the ice in a celebration like I had never witnessed before. The players threw their helmets, sticks and gloves in the air. They skated towards Chewy and wound up on the ice in one big pile of humanity. I shook Brian and Bob's hands and went on the ice. We shook hands with Marquette's team, and then headed to the Blue Line for the players to receive their UP district 8 Champion medals. Marquette received their runner up medals and then our team received theirs. Next, Judy Niemi presented our captains with the UP Championship trophy. Judy Niemi then came up to me and gave me an envelope with all the information for the state championship.

We lined up for pictures. It was a little difficult because of all of the equipment that was in the way. Right before we took pictures I stopped and looked. Tom wasn't in the team photo. I yelled to Tom to get to the picture, as he did. After our parents were done taking pictures I had an idea of Sarah taking a picture from above with our UP championship trophy. It was the perfect picture. I told Tom I wanted him to go to the State Championships with us. Tom was going to check with work but he said he wouldn't miss it for the world. I left the ice with Sarah and we went home in a state of bliss.

38

TIME TO WORK

That following Monday at practice, I told the players how proud I was of them, but we weren't done. It was now time to work harder than we had all season. The players looked nervous, but seemed to expect that we were going to pick it up a notch. I like doing our power skating and other techniques to work on speed and power. The players don't really care for these techniques, but they rarely argue about doing it. I think they noticed that their skating is gradually getting better and better.

We had 4 games coming up this next weekend and about 6 practices. The Bantams were playing in the states the weekend before us. We were working the same patterns with the Bantams as we were with the Squirts. Dave and Adam were doing an excellent job pushing the kids to their utmost potential. Our work wasn't just on the ice, it was off the ice as well. Each of the last few practices, the players were greeted with pizza when they were done.

After a few great practices I had some ideas on how we could better prepare for the states. I was pleased with the pace of our practices. Tom had been working with Chewy. Brian with the Forwards, Dave and Bob with the defense and I was bouncing around to each. It was starting to move like a perfect clock. The players were having sleep overs and hanging out with each other most of the season. I couldn't have been happier with the way our team was looking.

On Saturday February 26, we had Negaunee OK Industrial coming to town. Negaunee played us better than they had all season long and I was wondering how our team would react. We hit the ice and everything was perfect. Our warm up was more intense than it had been. The very first shift, Tyler scored with an assist from Hanna. Tyler's next shift he scored on a breakaway. We spent the first 10 minutes in Negaunee's zone. Tyler scored two more breakaways followed by Caleb scoring two in the last two minutes of the first period, assisted by Ethan and Sydnee. The First ended 6-0.

I was happy with our performance, but I didn't want to run up the score. I started switching players around and let some of the defensemen have some forward time. The second started and the first shift Brett received a pass from Caleb and shot it past Negaunee's goalie. The next shift, Nathan scored off Sydnee's pass to the front of the net. Nathan came back and scored again after he deflected a shot that Tommy made. We were up 8-0 with 9 minutes left in the second. I then had the players pass 5 times before shooting. Ethan deflected a Brett shot that found its way in the back of the net. With 42 seconds left Ethan scored again, after every player touched the puck, and the assists went to Sydnee and Tyler. The second ended 11-0.

I told the players not to score anymore, but to make a ton of passes. I wanted to work on dumping and changing. The game ended 11-0. I was pleased with our overall play. The second game was much of the same winning 12-0. We had to go to Iron River for our last games of the regular season. The wins against Negaunee gave us the CUP League Championship. It was also our, incredible 15th shutout of the season.

Sunday February 27, we went to Iron River for two games. Caleb Johnson wanted to talk to our players and show his State Championship medal to the players. I totally agreed to it. Caleb was a little nervous talking to a quiet room full of Polar Bears but he did an excellent job. Caleb told them, "Good luck and keep the championship in the UP". I thanked Caleb for sharing that with us and we finished getting ready for the game.

The team hit the ice and had another great warm up. The first period was deadlocked until Caleb scored the only goal of the first period. We started the second period on the power play and it didn't take long for Tyler to snap the net with an assist from CJ. Two minutes later Tyler scored again on a breakaway, making the game 3-0. Caleb and Nathan committed back to back penalties so we were down 5 on 3. Tyler, David, Brett, CJ and

Ethan did an excellent job killing off the penalties. It seemed to pick up our momentum and Caleb found the back of the net for his second of the game. Iron River got on a breakaway and found the back of the net making the game 4-1. A minute later Hanna scored on a nice pass from Nathan. With 25 seconds left, Caleb scored his third of the game with an assist from David, giving him the hat trick. We ended the second with a 6-1 lead.

The team went into the locker room with a nice amount of confidence. I left the locker room and let the kids listen to some music while the Zamboni resurfaced. We went back on the ice and Nathan took the faceoff. Nathan won the faceoff and Hanna passed it back to Nathan, who went down the ice and scored on a nice low shot. The game was now 7-1. The rest of the period Iron River had some nice runs up the ice that our defense stopped. The third ended and we won our 36th game of the season.

The players mostly stayed in the locker room in between games, listening to music and eating. I talked to Caleb Johnson between games, thanking him for talking to the players. I thought it was an incredibly nice thing to do. I then told him I was proud of him for playing hard and that his hard work is why he played AAA hockey in the summer. I went back into the locker room and told our players to get ready.

We went on the ice with Iron River and both teams looked crisp in their warm-ups. The first period didn't have many whistles. It was back and forth with both teams defense playing outstanding. The first ended with a 0-0 tie.

The second period was much of the same. The game remained 0-0 until 6:12 left in the second Nathan scored with an assist by Tyler. Caleb scored with two minutes left, assisted by Sydnee. Ethan scored 11 seconds later to make the game 3-0. With only a minute left, Caleb Johnson scored to cut the lead to 3-1. The second ended and we returned to the locker room for a resurface.

The players looked a little tired but they were in good spirits. Brian and Bob talked to the players about winning races to the puck and team passing. I told the players to get ready and we went out for the third period. About a minute into the third, Ethan broke free and scored our fourth goal of the game. Iron River committed a penalty with 7 minutes left. Caleb scored about a minute into the power play assisted by Tyler, making the game 5-1. A minute later Tyler scored with an assist from Hanna. The game would end 6-1 and we were 37-0. I couldn't have been any prouder of these players.

On the ride home I was talking to Sarah about her thoughts about trying to go undefeated or lose a game before we go to state. Sarah said that we shouldn't take fate out of the player's hands. I was caught between a rock and a hard place. Not losing a game would paint an even bigger target on us at state. After a lengthy discussion with Bob and Brian, and I decided to let the kids determine their own fate.

I had a parents, meeting the following Monday. I thanked the parents for their dedication and told them I appreciated all the fundraising they were doing and going to do. I then told the parents that there would be no more games accept for state so that the kids could try and get their undefeated season. I did make one stipulation, that nobody is going to talk about the undefeated season or post it on the internet. The parents agreed, and I was proud of them for doing so. It must have been hard for them to keep under wraps, something that we were all, so very proud of.

The real work was going to be done by both teams. The Squirts had three weeks until they played and the Bantams had two weeks. I felt bad for the Bantams because Zach Somero hurt his knee at a practice I was running. Zach had been having an awesome season and I had high hopes for him. Zach was going to come to state and cheer on his team. I know how hard this would be on him. This hurt our defense immensely because we needed every person to play to compete at the state level.

We had practice every day that week. We did some retention training to work on speed and strength. All of the coaches were precise and focused. All of the pegs were falling in the holes perfectly. Both teams had great skill and drive. I don't think there was anything that wasn't falling into place for both teams. The parents of both teams were feverishly working on any fundraiser that they could think of. Some of our local businesses were donating generously. Gabby Brunelle, who was a friend of Bob Heil's, was an awesome fundraiser. He helped out with some ideas and supported us.

Our two weeks of practice went by extremely fast. The Bantams were as ready as they could be. Jacob looked focused. Justin, Jonny, Kyle and Delaina were doing well and worked really hard. The players from Ontonagon looked good too. I wanted to talk to the captains Drew, Brady, Justin and Tony before our first game.

39

BANTAMS STATES

Sarah and I drove down to the state playoffs with Adam and Polly. We were set to take the 11 hour drive to Livonia. Adam drove all the way down and it gave me a chance to chat with Chewy and Jonny about what to expect at state. I had never personally been there as a coach or a player, but I had attended a few state championships. I knew the dedication that you had to have from player, parent, and coaches. I thought both sets of teams had this great combination.

On Friday March 11, we arrived at Livonia's rink for an introduction I will never forget. They had all the players go on the ice with their respective teams. Then they announced each player as we walked around the rink back to our teams waving at the fans as we walked by. The players name and numbers were announced as we walked around the ice rink. Eugene and I walked with Zach who was on crutches. I was so proud of Zach to come down with his team because I knew he was in anguish about not being able to play. The players received loud applause from the fans. After the festivities we returned to the hotel and prepared for the 6:00 pm game with Cadillac.

We got settled in at the hotel and returned to the rink. Before our game I walked to the other rink that was attached to the building to find some of my previous Tundra players in the Bantam AA state finals. Levi, Derek, Justin and Kyle were playing for Marquette. I walked back to the rink where we were playing to our locker room. The players were nervous and excited. I was very nervous. Dave and Adam were calm, cool and collected, as Dave had been at the state finals before.

The game started and our team speed was very good. Jacob was making some very nice saves. Cadillac scored first and took the lead a few minutes in. Justin countered with assists from Jonny and Tony. The first period would end 1-1. Dave told the players we had to make better passes and Adam chipped in with his own thoughts to just shoot the puck on net.

The second period we came out and took a quick lead with a goal from Drew assisted by Justin and Jonny. We then took a 2 goal lead with another goal from Justin assisted by Jonny and Logan. Cadillac didn't quit. They fought back with two goals in the final three minutes of the second period, tying the game.

In between periods Dave talked to the players about giving an effort. The players were not winning some of the battles that they should be. After a short resurface we hit the ice. It didn't feel like we had the momentum. Cadillac had scoring opportunities, but Kyle and Tony were doing a great job in front of the net. Jacob was making some nice saves. Cadillac, who was on a power play, scored with a few minutes left, giving them the lead 4-3. With a minute left Colton passed the puck up out of the zone to Brady, who passed it to a streaking Justin who came down the right side and shot it over the glove to tie the game with only 15 seconds left.

We went into overtime. Looking focused and now had the momentum. The first few minutes it was back and forth. After a scrum in front of Jacob, a Cadillac player shot it past Jacob who was screened. We had lost our first game, but we did show we didn't quit. We shook hands and went back to the hotel. There wasn't much to say the players did a good job. I hated the empty feeling, I had thought we could have done better.

March 12, 8:00 am, we were playing Southgate. I thought this game would be an interesting one. They had some nice shooters in their warm up, but we had ours too. The game started out on fire. Brady scored from outside the blue line on a pass from Tyler Behrendt. Southgate responded on back to back goals giving them the 2-1 lead. Justin got a pass from Drew and scored, tying the game. We went into the second period and I couldn't tell which way the game was going. It seemed both teams lacked defense as the score could rise. Southgate scored the next four goals and took a 6-2 lead towards the end of the second. Justin then scored his second goal of the game assisted, by Kyle. With seconds left, Brady took the puck up the ice and took a slap shot outside the blue line and put it over the goalie's blocker. This gave us some momentum going into the third.

One of the coaches from Ontonagon, Eugene Soumis, came into the locker room and tried to motivate the players. I wanted a chance to talk to the captains before we went back on the ice. I told Tony, Brady, Justin, and Drew, "To be a true leader of a team, means you do it with action, not with hollow words. You are the leaders this team needs and you will find yourselves victorious." The boys smiled and went onto the ice.

Southgate came out firing, trying to stop our momentum and did a good job by catching us off balanced on a bad shift change making the game 7-4. Then the Captains took over. We scored 5 unanswered goals. Justin scored on a breakaway, and then the next shift Brady took another slap shot that found its way in the back of the net. We then went on a power play after a Southgate penalty. In no time Brady tipped a Tony shot from the point. Justin scored a minute later on a nice pass from Tony. The scoring barrage didn't stop as Justin scored again off a rebound from a Brady slap shot. It was now 9-7 in our favor with only a few minutes left. Southgate brought it down and after a nice move they shot it behind Jacob to bring the game within one. After a time out Southgate pulled their goalie and Justin capitalized on it from a pass by Tony. The game ended 9-8 and it was probably one of the best come back wins I have ever been a part of.

In the locker room there was some gatorade, fiber bars, and other candy for the players after. The players feasted on them as I walked out of the rink and headed to the parking lot with Jonny who had a great game. We left and Adam had plans to go to Detroit to see the sites. We went to eat at the Hockey Town Café then we headed to Ford Field for a tour. We wanted to see Joe Louis arena so we drove there in hopes to see the rink. Adam sweet talked his way to getting us a tour. It was some place I had dreamed of going to. It was awesome how the old building was surrounded by tradition and history. I was overjoyed to see the new football field and the old hockey rink all in the same day.

We headed back to the hotel for a short stay and we were back to the rink to face off against home town Livonia. We went on the ice and Brady was having some stomach problems. We asked Brady what he ate. Brady responded, "Nothing but those protein bars." I asked if they had a brown wrapper. Brady said, "yes." I told Brady, "Those weren't protein bars they were fiber bars!" It wasn't 30 seconds later Dave was assisting Brady to hurry and get to the locker room. Adam and I looked at Brady and Dave running to open the locker room as we hoped they would get the door opened in time.

We started the game without Brady. It didn't take long for Tyler to put us on the score board with assists from Kyle and Justin. Livonia didn't waste any time coming back and tying it 1-1 at the end of the first period. We were slowing down and making some errors, but we were hanging in tough.

We started the second slow and Livonia capitalized on 3 goals. Down by 3 going into the third Dave tried to motivate the players, but for some reason the kids weren't responding. We gave up 2 more goals and lost 6-1. We found out after the game that we didn't make it to Sunday's semifinals. We had missed it by one goal. I told the players, "It was a great season, but it is not over we still might get in, proud of you all." I shook the player's hands and left the locker room.

I had a very disturbing feeling come over me. I was disappointed in the way some of our team played. I don't think we played as well as we could of. I knew that some players gave everything they had. The players looked devastated in the locker room when they were told of our unfortunate fate. We had lost on a tiebreaker by one goal and were heading home on Sunday.

The ride home was very quiet. I knew Johnny was disappointed, but I was proud of him. He played very well all weekend long. Sometimes fate is out of control and you just have to deal with the hand you are dealt. I started to think about the Squirts going to Cadillac next Thursday. I was coming up with a plan for Mondays practice.

I had an idea. I wanted to get some of my old players to scrimmage against the Squirts. Jacob, Jonny, Justin, Caleb Greenough, Alex Jones, Gavin Mattson were all asked to come to this practice and pick up the tempo. We also had a few last year Mites come and play against the Squirts. I set it up for an hour and a half practice no body checking. I wanted the versatility so the players could find a way to succeed. The challenge would be fun to watch.

TRAGEDY FOR THE SQUIRTS

I went to work Monday March 15 in a great mood and ready for some hockey. I walked through the prison entry doors to a quiet staff. I wasn't sure what was going on but it didn't seem like anything good. As I walked down the hall and relieved the midnight shift officer I was quickly informed that Ray Brunelle's dad, Gabby, had passed away. Gabby had been one of our biggest supporters for our team.

I immediately had a sad and somber feeling come over me. I was devastated by the news. I felt sad as could be fighting off the tears while I thought of Ray and Bob's family. It then struck me that this could not only affect my friends but this could affect our team. I knew that this was a bad thing no matter how you would look at it. Losing Gabby was not only terrible for my friends, but it was bad for the surrounding community as well.

After work I went home and talked to Sarah about the tragedy. Sarah was shocked and was concerned about Ray and his family. I had to focus and keep my nose to the grindstone. I spent a few hours thinking of how the team could honor Gabby. The way I think I coped with losing him was to keep the kids focused and get the kid's minds back on hockey. This practice was going to go well and the players were going to be too busy to think of anything else.

I went to the rink and got the benches ready, filled the water bottles and put the pucks on the ice. My mind was still wandering and I found it difficult to concentrate. I could hear Gabby giving me an earful about how Bob and I stunk as coaches and we were lucky to have great players. He would joke about this every time he saw me. I was going to miss his humor and his love of the kid's sports. I knew I needed to get my act straight and prepare the kids.

After all the players arrived I separated the locker rooms and talked to each group of players to address the guidelines. I told the players there was no messing around, but have fun. I then reminded the older players that there were no slap shots or checking as there was at their level. The players on both teams were in a good mood and wanted to play some hockey. We were going to do a warm up and then go right to playing some hockey.

As the players walked out I saw Brett and pulled him aside just to give him a hug to let him know I was thinking of him. Brett and Gabby were buddies and I wanted Brett to stay focused. I knew in time this would be behind him.

We went on the ice and the players who showed up were very happy to play. Austin Trier, Nick Garnell, Jack Santini, Zach Baross, and Brayden Bender came to help out from our mite team. I thought the Squirts would get the hardest challenge that they had all year long. I told Jacob to make it very hard for them to score and play them tough. I then went to the forwards, Johnny, Justin, Caleb and Gavin and told them to be really hard on Tyler, Caleb, Ethan and Nathan. I wanted them to work hard. I was worried about someone getting hurt, but Brian put my mind at ease by telling me, they play together all the time.

We started playing with a pace that we hadn't played at all year long. The forwards were getting a work out that I think they didn't expect. The forwards fought back hard and did a really good job. CJ, Brett, Tommy and Travis were doing a solid job clearing the puck and covering in front of the net. Every aspect of playing players from our own organization gave me a great feeling of accomplishment. Some of the players were not playing in our polar bear organization because we didn't have a Pee Wee team. It was good to know that they would always be Polar Bears.

After an excellent practice and seeing our Squirt team compete with the older players, I knew they were ready for any and all challenges they would face at state. Every player left the ice smiling and enjoying their time together again. The parents had bought pizza for all the kids and we enjoyed our last team meal before we went down state.

We had one last practice on Tuesday and we were not going to work too hard. I wanted to just stretch our legs and mentally prepare for the weekend. We used the time to give the kids nothing but positive comments. We let the kids do some shooting and passing and our short practice was over. It also gave the team time to be reminded to take all of their equipment and prepare for Fridays game against Tawas, Michigan.

THE JOURNEY TO CADILLAC

We met early in Ironwood to take a Bus down to Cadillac. All the family members were on board and everyone had a nervous excitement. I found out that morning that the parents had something special planned after we left Ironwood. Everyone was accounted for and I said good bye and thank you to Lou from the Ironwood Info.com, Lou had been very supportive of our team and followed us all season taking pictures and posting our articles for every game.

As we left the parking lot we were escorted by the Police and Fire departments with sirens screaming in the air. We got onto US highway 2 and saw that the side roads were filled with people wishing us good luck with signs and waves. The players were glued and amazed at all of the attention they had received. They knew everyone in the area was supporting us, but I never expected this. I know it was a moment the kids would never forget and it sent them off to state with and obvious momentum.

We went down the highway and through Bessemer with our police escort to Wakefield. We slowed down in Wakefield and turned into an open area next to a café. There were about 25 people there waiting for us. It was Ray Brunelle and his family. The parents had paid for a banner that said "Ironwood Polar Bear Squirts District 8 UP champions 2010-2011" and on the bottom of the banner it said "In Honor of Gabby". Everyone was excited.

I walked over by the parents and the players took the banner and lined up for a picture. Each player and sibling was given a balloon to release all at once in honor of Gabby. The daily globe and Lou from ironwood info were there to take pictures. It was one of the most heartfelt things I had ever seen done. The parents counted down 5-4-3-2-1 and the kids released the balloons into the air. A few tears came down my face and I gave Ray a hug and went back onto the bus. After everyone was back on the bus Brian played a Mighty ducks movie and we left for Cadillac.

We drove through the Upper Peninsula and made a pit stop in Escanaba for some food. It was nice to stop and see the players having fun. We got back on the bus and left for out next designation. Sarah and I wanted Warner and Gabriel Young to be on this trip. The parents were more than agreeable with my request. I wanted Warner to be there to see his old team and his old friends play. Warner was totally excited, as was Gabriel. We arrived at a crossing near Newberry and picked the kids up. Warner was met with hugs from his team mates and some of the parents. Gabriel was very excited and Sarah and Polly were talking her ears off. It had been way too long since these friends had been together.

We left and our destination was the Mackinaw Bridge. We stopped in St. Ignace for a break. The players had one last chance to stretch their legs and get a bite to eat. After our short break, it was time to continue to Cadillac. I sat by myself and mentally prepared for the weekend in front of our team. I was ready and so were the players.

STATE CHAMPIONSHIP PLAYOFFS

We arrived in Cadillac after a very long trip we exited the bus and unloaded to our hotel. The hotel was ready for us and they were very accommodating. It was only an hour when a few of us wanted to go to the rink and find out where it was. George, our bus driver was excellent all weekend long and took us to the rink. We found the rink with no problem and returned to the hotel.

I walked room to room and made sure I talked to each player about getting enough rest and eating something. Each player looked so focused. I was astounded at the players and their dedication as it continued to thrive. I talked with Bob and Brian before I went back to my room. Both coaches looked pretty relaxed and I think we're feeling on top of the world. I went back to the room and called it an early night.

I woke up early in the morning and walked around an empty hotel. It gave me time to prepare our players to do their team building. We were going to do a warm up and get mentally prepared for our one and only game of the day. I also wanted to go to the rink and check out some of the early games and see what we were up against. I asked Sarah to make sure the kids were relaxing and eating something. We found George in the lobby and asked if he could give us a ride to the rink to see the first two games and he gladly agreed.

A few of us went to the rink around 11:30. Cadillac was playing St. Clair Shores and both teams had some nice skaters. After the game, we stayed to see Livonia and Westland play. I was sitting with Jeff Baxter talking about what we thought of all 4 teams that we had seen, when one parent from Livonia approached Jeff and I who in the bleachers. He was a really big guy. He asked Jeff if we were from Ironwood. Jeff looked back at him and stated, "Yes." The man then asked," I can't find any losses for you on the internet." Jeff just looked at me and shrugged his shoulders. I had told the parents no talking about our team record. The man who looked agitated, and then said in a stern voice, "Are you undefeated? That is a yes or no question." I then butted in and stated back to him, "YA." The man then turned around and said to a buddy who was waiting at the bottom of the bleachers and said, "Yup, they haven't lost, but there isn't much competition in the UP."

I looked at Jeff and jokingly said, "Oops I broke my own rule." I chuckled, but I was angered by his arrogance and thought, he will see our team soon enough. We left the rink to go back and prepare the team. I was now full of energy and ready to play. The adrenaline was pumping the whole ride back to the hotel.

We got the players together for some sprints and some jumping. The players were quiet but they were focused on the task at hand. We then did some stretching with some mental exercises. After we were done we had a team breakdown. I then told the players to go get their bags and sticks and let's go have some fun. The players got their equipment and got on the bus.

We drove to the rink and it was quiet on the bus. I had brought my MP 3 player to help me with my nerves. I listened to the music while the players were getting ready for our 3:30 game with Tawas. My thoughts were only of the players and keeping them motivated. Brian looked really pumped up and was smiling, ready to get started. Bob was quiet and looked intense. Tom didn't want to go on the bench I think he just wanted to keep things the same as they were at Districts. We walked into the arena and walked past the State Championship plaque and the individual medals. The players went to the locker room and started to get ready.

It was game time. I walked into the locker room and had CJ stop the music while I said a few things before we went on the ice. I told the players. "Today is like any other day. I don't care about what players on their team we needed to watch. I care about one thing having fun, this is your time enjoy it. You earned it." ARE YOU READY?" The players Responded with a thunderous, "YA!" Bob opened the locker room door and the kids exited the locker room down the hall and waited for me at the door to the arena.

The parents were lining up and clapping, waiting for the Polar Bears to come out. The music was loud and started to get my adrenaline pumping again. I told Chewy to have fun and be a leader. I asked one last time, "Polar Bears are you ready?" The players screamed, "YA!" I opened the door and the players walked through the gauntlet of family and friends patting them on the back as they passed them to the ice door. I looked to my right and there was Hank and Jeff Bailey who came down from Ontonagon to see us play. I gave Hank and Warner a high five as we walked to the bench.

After we had a great warm up, Tyler asked to go shake hands with the opposing coaches. The players were ready and we went to center ice to get the game underway. Brett and the other players wanted to pay a tribute to Gabby. I told the referees to tell their coach about it so they would understand what was going on. The players went around the center ice circle and skated in a circle with their index finger pointed to the ice then in single file they went towards the camera at center ice and pointed to the sky. Now it was game time.

We wanted fast shifts and quick changes to start the game. About a minute in Caleb scored on a Tawas defensive turnover making the game 1-0. We were skating really well and so was Tawas. They were a nice group of skaters. Four minutes in, Tawas committed a penalty. Brian set up our power play line. A minute in Caleb scored his second of the game with an assist from Ethan for a power play goal. A minute and a half later Tyler got a breakaway and put it past Tawas's goalie making the game 3-0. The rest of the period was even and Tawas had a few good opportunities that Chewy turned away. Our defense was playing tough and making nice passes.

The second period started with us on a penalty kill after Tyler got called for a hooking penalty. A minute in Tawas scored a power play goal on us. It was only the second power play goal we allowed all season long. A few minutes later we went back on the power play after a holding penalty. Tyler took the faceoff and Nathan passed it to Ethan, who passed it back to Tyler. Tyler took the shot and beat the goalie glove side, making the game 4-1. Three minutes later Tyler scored his third of the game with assists from Caleb and Ethan. Forty five seconds later Caleb broke free on another breakaway and scored making the game 6-1. Tawas was not quitting, they ran the puck down and broke free of our defense and scored with 3 minutes left. The score would remain unchanged at 6-2 end of the second.

We went to the locker room and there wasn't much to change. It was a great game thus far and our legs looked solid. We went back to the arena after a quick resurface. I figured Tawas would come out on fire, and they did. A few minutes in Tawas scored with some nice passing. Tawas had some momentum and were in our zone steady. They were giving us problems, but Chewy was making some saves that we needed. Tawas scored again with 6 and a half minutes left. The game was now 6-4. Our players were starting to dig a little deeper. Their skating was even with Tawas. The game was going back and forth until Tawas called a time out with a minute and a half left. I saw some of our players were tired and I told them to sit down because I was calling a time out so we could get a longer rest. The coaches were being really positive and letting the players know that there was only a minute and a half left to give it their all. Right off the face off Caleb took the puck and bumped it off the glass then shot it in the empty net for his third goal to seal the game 7-4.

We shook hands and I had a great feeling of admiration of the Tawas team that never quit. I talked to the coaches and told them it was a great game. I told them to be proud of those kids, "They are a class act and they play like it too." They congratulated us and told us good luck the rest of the tournament. We walked in the locker room and told the players good game. I told them I was proud of them for not giving up. We reminded the players to hydrate and get ready to play. The locker room was exciting, the players were jamming out to music enjoying the moment.

We arrived to the hotel and Sarah said the kids looked really good. I thought Tawas was a very solid team. I was totally exhausted and knew we were playing the Livonia team next.

We woke up that Saturday morning and had our team breakfast. The players were in a good mood. We did our warm up and stretching. I was feeling a little bit more confident after seeing the kids play so well. Bob thought we were playing well, but Livonia wasn't going to be a pushover. I agreed. Brian told me that we should go with the diamond if we got the chance.

We went to the rink and were playing at 11:30. The players were jamming out to the music and getting ready. This gave me a chance to mingle with Jeff Bailey and see what he thought. Jeff said we had a good chance and that we passed really well. I was happy to hear a good report from him.

I went back to the locker room and told the kids it was time to turn it up a notch. We left the locker room and waited at the entry door of the arena. The parents were there like clockwork, waiting for their Polar Bears. The kids were pumped and I opened the door. The players walked with confidence down the rubber mat to the ice. The players were flying on the ice. It was our best warm up all season long.

Across from the bench Hanna's, Aunt Kristy, Baross was setting up her laptop so we could live stream the remaining games. The players all knew they were on. We were excited to get going. The players went around Chewy for a team pep talk. Brian gave the players one last word, "Play hard."

We went to the faceoff circle and immediately Livonia was in our offensive zone. We had to make some adjustments at first, but we settled in. the rest of the period was deadlocked. We got called for two penalties back to back. Ethan got called on the first, which David and Nathan did an excellent job killing it off. The second, CJ got called for a tripping call with 3 minutes left in the first. A Livonia player broke free on a breakaway and Chewy stoned him cold. After the whistle two Livonia players were using there sticks underneath Chewy trying to pry the puck loose. I made sure the players knew that I was displeased with the extra digging on Chewy. Tyler took the next faceoff and won it to Ethan, who passed it to a streaking Tyler. The diamond had worked and Tyler took it down and scored high blocker side for a shorthanded goal. At the end of the period Livonia committed a tripping penalty with a minute left and we went into the second period with a power play.

In between periods we calmed the players down and told them one thing. "Win your battles." The players looked really intense and our defense was playing solid. We went to the faceoff circle and Tyler won the faceoff to Hanna, who passed it back to Tyler. Tyler made a slip move past the defenseman and took a hard shot that snapped the back of the net giving us a 2-0 lead on a power play goal. The next line change Ethan won the faceoff to CJ, who skated it up and passed it off to Caleb, who scored on a nice wrist shot.

After scoring the goal Brett approached me and told me something I will never forget. He said, "Coach Gabby was my friend. I want to score a goal for him." I put my hand on top of Brett's head and said, "You got it." I called Tyler, Nathan and Sydnee over to me. I then called Tommy from the defensive side to hear what I was telling the next line out. I said, "This is what we are going to do. Tyler wins the puck and brings it back to Brett. Nathan and Sydnee will go up the ice with Brett once he has the puck. Tyler, you will drop back and cover for Brett. Brett, if you lose the puck get open and we will get it back to you." We were going on the power play and I knew this was going to work.

The kids were ready and with eight and a half minutes left in the second it worked according to plan. Brett went into our zone and brought the puck out of the zone. Tyler dropped back to cover for Brett. Brett made some nice stickhandling moves past the defenseman and shot it top shelf, "Where Mommy hides the cookies." Instead of celebrating, Brett went in front of Kristy's lap top, took his right index finger and pointed to the sky where Gabby was probably celebrating. As Brett came off the ice he was greeted by his dad who gave him a big hug.

The next few minutes were a little rough. Livonia wasn't happy about being down 4-0. The game was getting chippy. Ethan's line came out with 3 minutes left in the second. They took the faceoff and passed it around Livonia like we did most of the season. Brett passed to Caleb from the point then passed it to a wide open Ethan on the back door who buried it past Livonia's goaltender. We were getting steady pressure on Livonia and with 1:49 left Ethan got a breakaway after passes from Caleb and Hanna. Ethan took it down and deked the goalie making the game 6-0. The second period remained unchanged and we went into the locker room for a resurface.

As I was walking, Sarah and Polly came up to me. Sarah said that the Livonia parents were acting like a bunch of jerks. She told me that if they left the stands that they would take their jackets and purses and throw them over the bleachers. One parent even would stand in front of the laptop blocking view of the ice. I told Sarah to have the parents keep their cool and this game would be over soon. I reminded her to tell the parents that they were representing the Polar Bear organization.

This wasn't surprising to me since that some of the parents from Livonia had already shown their arrogance. The players on the ice were getting more and more aggressive. I went to the locker room and let Bob and Brian know what was going on in the stands. Our focus was going to stay on the ice. I told the tournament director about the childish behavior going on in the stands and if he would keep an eye on it.

I went back in the locker room and told the players a few of my concerns. The first concern was that I didn't care about the score but I did care about the extra sticks that were on Chewy when he was freezing the puck. The second was our defensive coverage. I wanted the players to pick up a player and take away the pass. The last thing was, have some fun and don't worry about what their players are saying or doing on the ice. Play a clean and good hockey game. Chewy was having one of the best games of the year.

We went back to the arena for the third period. The first half was deadlocked with Livonia getting a few scoring opportunities. Nathan and David helped kill off consecutive penalties by Caleb and Travis. They received the penalties for interference because they were trying to stop the Livonia players from digging on Chewy. At the 5 minute mark a Livonia player was digging again on Chewy when Caleb flew in too fast and body checked him. Caleb received a double minor penalty. I asked the referee about the extra digging and that we were only trying to protect our goalie. The Livonia player was hurt on the play so we received the penalties.

A little while later David got called for hooking and we were down 5 on 3. Livonia pulled their goalie with 4 minutes left. The next play was one of the best I have ever seen. Nathan took the faceoff and won it to CJ, who iced the puck. Nathan was after the puck hard. Nathan won control of the puck and all 6 Livonia players were trying to get the puck. Nathan was playing keep away and winning. For 45 seconds Nathan kept the puck in the zone and even had two scoring opportunities with no goalie in net. After Livonia finally got the puck from an exhausted Nathan, they quickly brought it up the ice.

Tyler was waiting to go on the ice and change for a tired Nathan. Before Nathan could get to the bench a Livonia player shot the puck at Chewy and the 6 players who all went to the net were just too much. CJ and Brett did their best to try to clear it, but one player knocked it free and put it past Chewy.

It was our third power play goal allowed all season long. We were still shorthanded. It was now 5 on 4. Ethan pushed the face off past Livonia's center and split the defense taking it in and shooting it high past the goalie for our second shorthanded goal of the game. Nathan took the faceoff in our zone and won it to Ethan. Nathan and Ethan passed it back and forth and made it past the Livonia defense. Nathan gave a nice pass to Ethan who shot it low five hole to make the game 8-1. I told the players to try not to score any more and dump it in.

Tyler took the puck down and dumped it in. A player from Livonia tried to pass it out but Tyler picked it off and passed it to Hanna, who was in front of the net. Hanna hit the puck out of midair and put it in the net with only a minute left. With 30 seconds left Tommy got called on a tripping call and then a scrum happened where Tyler got locked up and both players would finish the game in the penalty box for un-sportsman's like conduct. I wanted the puck out of the zone, so we set up the diamond again. I figured with 30 seconds left that we could ice the puck easier. Ethan won the faceoff to Nathan who dumped it off the glass and out of our zone. Ethan won the race to the puck and brought it in and scored his second shorthanded goal of the game with 7 seconds left.

We won the game 10-1. We shook hands and left the ice. As we walked off the ice I saw the big parent from Livonia who had nothing to say. I just walked by a quiet group of parents and didn't say a word. Our parents were behind them cheering for our players yelling, "Good Game." "Proud of you." Warner and Hank asked if they could come in the locker room. I agreed. There wasn't too much to say but I was so proud of our kids. They proved to everyone that they were not thinking of anything other than playing as hard as they could. The locker room was unusually quiet, I think they were starting to feel the confidence.

I exited to the lobby where I saw the tournament director. I thanked him for looking out for our fans. I shook his hand and went to the bus. We had an 8:00 PM game with Westland. On the bus I reminded the players to rehydrate and take it easy. I went back to our room and laid down for a little bit.

A few hours had past and we met up for our pre-game exercise. The players were totally focused. I think a little part of them was thinking of Gabby and not focused on any of the wrong things, like scoring hat tricks.

I was proud of them and I knew that our team was giving the best effort each and every shift. We got on the bus and took our short journey to the Wex arena.

The players got ready like they always did, CJ playing the music they wanted to listen to and a little singing here and there from the players. The ice was done and we walked out to the entry door of the arena. The players walked out to the bright arena with the cheers from our parents and fans. I was excited because with a win we could have 1st seed and we would be in the semifinals.

After the warm up and a pep talk by Chewy and the captains the game was ready to start. Tyler took the face off and after a few seconds broke free on a breakaway. Tyler took the puck down the middle and shot it high blocker giving us an early 1-0 lead. We then had to kill off back to back penalties. David did an excellent job with Ethan killing them off. Our defense was playing solid and was giving Westland difficulty getting a high quality shot. Matthew was making nice saves again helping the team to gain confidence. With a minute left in the first Brett skated the puck up the ice and passed it to Ethan. Ethan skated it in and passed it to Caleb who shot it low and hard to beat Westland's goalie. The first period came to an end with a 2-0 lead.

The 2nd started and Westland didn't waste any time when a player got past our defense and scored two minutes in. A few minutes later Ethan scored off a nice pass from Caleb. We were gaining momentum. A few minutes after that, Hanna scored off a pass from Tyler. With the game now 4-1 the coach of Westland came unglued. He was yelling at the referee's and giving them a hard time. He received a game misconduct and bench minor. The referees came to our bench to tell me what penalties they were going to receive. I asked the referee to not take it out on the kids and I didn't want any more penalties on Westland. I felt it was unfair to the kids who were doing their best on the ice.

The rest of the second got a little chippy with the Westland players. I felt like they were losing their composure like their coach did. There wasn't any more scoring in the second, but Westland players were trying their best to come back. We went in the locker room for the resurface intermission.

I walked in the locker room and noticed that Chewy was angry. I asked him what was wrong and he stated, "I wanted to get a shutout for Gabby."

I said to him, "Chewy, you are having a great weekend. Don't worry about shutouts or bad goals. Just worry about having fun. Keep up the good work." I felt like there was some pressure and I needed to address it. I told the kids, "Gabby isn't going to care if you win or lose. I know it's great to win, but we are all here because we love the game. Play your heart out and great things will happen." I then put on the music and walked out to the hallway and talked with Bob and Brian.

The resurface was complete and we went onto the ice for the third period. The kids didn't say much. They just wanted to get the game going. Tommy got called on a tripping penalty only 9 seconds in. Brian set up the diamond and our penalty kill went out on the ice. Right off the faceoff Caleb pushed it between Westland's defenders and took it all the way and buried it behind their goalie. The shorthanded goal gave us some momentum. With 5 minutes left Westland started to lose their composure. They committed a really bad checking penalty. Towards the end of the power play Tyler got the puck off a turnover and buried it past Westland's goalie. After another Westland penalty with only 20 seconds left Travis scored off a pass from Ethan.

Westland's coach called a time out. I called everyone over and told them that their coach was probably telling them good game, and be good sports. I told the players to shoot the puck in their corner and let the time run out. I was wrong. The faceoff was at center ice. Ethan took the faceoff and won it to Brett. Brett passed it to Ethan, who shot it in the corner just like I asked them to. As Brett passed the puck a player came after him and kneed him, trying to injure him. Brett went to the ice and immediately held his right knee. Bob was screaming. I couldn't believe that this was happening. With a few seconds left I ran on to the ice to check on Brett.

As I got to Brett I heard screaming from the crowd. I looked up and the fans were pointing in the corner where Ethan was lying motionless. My heart stopped. I sprinted to Ethan. Tom Kangas was already in the corner with him. Tom said with tears in his eyes, "One of their players cross checked him from behind, head first in the boards." An incredible anger rose in me. I focused on Ethan talking to him. I pinched his leg and he responded. I was relieved a little, but I was still angry. Brian came up and was lying on the ice next to Ethan talking to him. I asked Brian what he said as I wiped the tears from my eyes. Brian said, "He feels his legs."

I looked up and saw Westland's team standing together looking at us. The referee said if we didn't want to shake hands he would understand. I said, "We will shake hands for the honor of the game, not for them." Brian was on Ethan's right side and Tom and I were on his left. The arena was eerily quiet. Brian asked Ethan if he could get up. Ethan said yes. As Ethan arose there was thunderous applause from our fans. We helped Ethan to center ice where the handshake always starts.

We shook hands and the coach said something to me about having had problems with those kids all season long. I just grasped his hand and said, "That was the most atrocious thing I have ever seen in my life." We left the ice and went to the locker room. After the players settled down I wanted to talk to them. I said, "Listen up, we do not play like that. We will succeed at anything we do because we play fair and we play hard. That team is going home. We sent them there. I am proud of you."

I went to the lobby where I told the parents to get on the bus. The parents were concerned due to some snide comments about our players being babies and didn't want to see them get any more verbal abuse. Sarah told me Kasey Lundin was crying because a parent was swearing at her. I just told them to go on the bus and I would take care of everything. I noticed the state police had arrived and I knew what I was going to do.

I went back to the locker room and told the players we were exiting as a team. I asked Brian to lead us and Bob to follow us. As we exited there was nothing but silence from the lobby, which was full of Westland parents. As Bob exited the door and our team was out and on the bus I chatted with the tournament director. He said, "I am sorry." I replied, "We are coming here tomorrow and going to win this tournament. I am in shock at how these people play down here." I then turned towards the Westland parents and stared at them as they all looked away. I know I had a hateful look in my eyes. I was never that angry in all my life.

We went back to the hotel and the parents were quiet and somber. Warner was still upset. I told him that kids who play hockey like that go nowhere. "Play this game right and the right thing will happen for you." I gave Warner a hug and he went and sat with Tyler. As Warner left he said, "Scotty that's my team too." I nodded my head and smiled at him.

We went to the hotel and I couldn't settle down. I was still fighting mad. I went to Bob's room to see how Brett's knee was feeling. Brett smiled and said it hurt, but it was feeling better. I was relieved to hear that. As I walked to check on Ethan I couldn't help but think what they were thinking. What kind of a coach sends kids to do something so diabolical and evil. I got to Ethan's room and Brian answered the door. I asked how he was doing. Brian invited me in and I saw Ethan lying in bed. I asked Ethan how he was doing. Ethan replied, "I've got a headache." I told him to take it easy. He was checked by medical personnel and didn't seem to have a concussion.

I went back to our room and noticed that Caleb, Warner, Tyler CJ, Chewy, and Nathan were all going room to room to check on how the boys were doing. I went back to the room and stopped by Adam and Polly's room. Sarah was in the room with them talking when Adam turned and said to me, "Relax, stay focused for tomorrow. The kids are playing excellent." I agreed and went back to relax. I went to sleep, but the echoes of the arena were haunting me.

I woke up hoping to feel better, but I didn't. I was still angry. I knew I had to bury this strong feeling. I went down for breakfast early and sat alone for a little while. I started to write down what was happening, when George our bus driver joined me for some breakfast. George said, "Do only what you can control. Those kids are a tough bunch. They play with a lot of heart." I replied, "Yes they do. I am proud of them." After the kids were showing up one by one I decided we were only going to do some stretching due to our injuries.

It was time to go to the arena again. I wasn't sure who we were playing, but I didn't care. Our Polar Bears were playing as well as they had all season long. We got on the bus and the kids were quiet but confident. They walked to their assigned locker room and started to get ready. Each time they walked past the table with the medals and the state championship plaque you could see a glance from each of them. I wanted it bad for them.

It was game time, there wasn't anything to say, but to just let them be and do what they do best. We did our routine with a solid warm up and sportsmanship, with a handshake of the opposing coaches. Holland Michigan was our opponent. I thought we matched up evenly when I saw them play. All of our players were healed up and ready to play.

Tyler took the opening faceoff and pushed it past the center and split the defense. Tyler skated hard and scored to start the game. Holland came back and Chewy stoned them on back to back scoring opportunities. The rest of the period was tight, until Ethan scored with a minute and a half left assisted by Sydnee. The next shift Holland committed a tripping penalty. Tyler won the face off to Brett who skated it up the ice. Brett shot the puck and Hanna scored a power play goal off the rebound with 31 seconds left. The first period ended with us up 3-0. Tommy and Travis were playing outstanding defense.

The second period was a deadlock. Holland's goalie made some really nice saves to keep us off the scoreboard. Chewy was doing the same making some great saves and excellent play by the defensemen. CJ and Brett were doing an awesome job at protecting Chewy and clearing the puck. The second period would end the same score as the first, 3-0.

This was becoming a great game. I walked into the locker room and smiled at the players I walked over to the CD player next to CJ and turned the music on. I left the locker room to the hallway where Brian and Bob were waiting. We wanted the kids to enjoy the moment. They were winning most of their battles and they looked like they were having fun. After the ice was done Bob walked in and told the players, "Let's go! The ice is ready." The players ran onto the ice. We knew they were ready and having fun. I didn't want to over coach.

The third period started and Holland came out on fire. They had a few scoring opportunities, but our defensive coverage, along with Chewy playing well was too much for Holland. Each team killed off two penalties in the middle of the period. With 3:41 left in the game Holland committed a tripping penalty. It only took 20 seconds for Nathan to feed Tyler in front of the net for our fourth goal of the game and our second power play goal of the game. The game ended 4-0. Chewy had fulfilled his wish and pointed to the sky for Gabby and we advanced to the championship game.

The parents had a nervous look about them as we went onto the bus. I was very nervous, but in some ways I wasn't. I had never been so confident in a team. I wasn't confident that we could beat anyone, but that we could compete with anyone. This group proved all season long they refused to quit.

We went to eat at a local diner and sat down as a team. The players were chatting and laughing and enjoying their time together. After we ate I had a plan to go back to the hotel where we had a conference room set up so the kids could rest and watch movies. The players all lined up and got ready to watch the movie. I had been planning for months to show it to them. The movie was Youngblood. I watched it every night before a game. I edited it so the kids could watch it. Some of the players had seen it, but it was a great way to waste time since we had to wait a few hours before we played. While the movie was playing I sent some parents to get some Gatorade for the next game. You could see the players picturing themselves as the star player. Chatting amongst them about what a sweet shot it was. After the movie was over I said, "Picture yourself scoring that goal. Think of the feeling of being on the bench during a championship game. Now let's go and make it happen." The players ran to the bus and we left one last time for the Wex Arena.

The players entered the locker room quietly. I told CJ to put the music on. I then walked out into the hallway and put my MP3 player on full blast. My nerves were kicking. I tried to call Eric Boyer and ask for some pointers, but there was no answer. I sat there as I thought about all the things these kids accomplished. Not the records, but the team work they have done. I was proud of them. I had a tear in my eye looking out the window when Brian tapped me on the left arm and said it was time.

We walked in the locker room and I yelled as loud as I could, "WHAT TIME IS IT?" The players stood up and screamed, "GAMETIME!" I opened the door and they exited and waited for me to open the door to the arena. My phone was vibrating from all of the good luck text messages everyone was sending me. I opened the door to screaming fans and family's. Hank was right at the door with Warner to be the first to give their good luck to the team.

We hit the ice and I took a deep breath. I thought to myself, now it was time to work, we were playing hometown Cadillac. They were a speedy team that could move the puck. I thought they were pretty good. After announcing both teams we had one last breakdown. I said, "You worked for this moment, right here right now. Bring it. Everything you got. Leave everything here." The players broke it down 1-2-3 Polar Bears.

We went to the faceoff circle ready. Tyler was ready with Nathan at wing and Hanna at his other wing. CJ was paired with Travis. The puck dropped and both teams were very careful with the puck. The game was at a stalemate when a Cadillac player shot the puck from the point and put it behind a screened Chewy. We were down 1-0. The next shift we loaded up our power line. It only took 23 seconds and Tyler passed it to Nathan, who passed it to Ethan, who buried it past Cadillac's goalie tying the game. The rest of the period was a stalemate. It ended 1-1.

We went into the second and I told the players to keep it up and pass more. We started the second like the first, back and forth. The period was filled with solid defense. CJ, Brett, Travis and Tommy were playing awesome. I was very proud of them taking the angle and blocking shots. There were a few loud pipes that caused the fans to gasp for some air. Cadillac was playing tough defense too. They were double shifting players, but I wasn't going to do that because I knew if we kept up playing like we were they would wear out. The second ended tied at 1-1.

The players were slowing down on both sides. I had an idea. I had Jim Collins and Tom get the Gatorade we bought during the movie. We filled half the water bottles and I told the players to drink up the Gatorade and their legs would come back stronger than ever. The players believed it and drank the Gatorade. Brian and Bob were talking to individual players being supportive and helping build confidence.

I called the players in a huddle and told them for the first time," We are not a team. We are a family. Play your hearts out; leave everything on the ice." We took the faceoff and Brett stopped one of Cadillac's players and passed the puck to Caleb. Caleb made a move and took it towards the net and shot it behind their goalie to give us a 2-1 lead 14 seconds in. the next shift, Brett passed it to Tyler who was in full stride. Tyler broke free and shot it past Cadillac's goalie. A few minutes later Tyler scored again with an assist from Ethan. Two minutes later Cadillac committed a high stick penalty. Brian stacked the power play line. Nathan stole the puck from Cadillac's center and passed it to Tyler. Tyler turned on the speed and blew past a defenseman and shot it past the goalie for the hat trick.

With 5 minutes left you could feel the energy. I chose to do something we hadn't done all year long. We were going to play defense. David, Hanna and Sydnee were going to chase the puck. Tyler, Caleb, Ethan and Nathan were going to play to intercept the puck in the neutral zone. They did exactly like I asked them to. Cadillac didn't have any more scoring opportunities and before you knew it there were 10 seconds left. The parents counted 10-9-8-7-6-5-4-3-2-1.

The thunderous cheering and yelling was deafening. I watched as if in slow motion the players toss their sticks, then their gloves, and last their helmets. They skated towards Chewy and tackled him by his crease. Brian and Bob met me in the middle of the bench for a big hug. "We did it!" was all I could say. The referee skated by and threw me the game puck and skated away. We went out on the ice with our arms in the air. We told the kid's they did and awesome, job clapping for them as the parents chanted 42 and 0. We shook hands with Cadillac and the kids skated to their parents who were coming on the ice.

Chewy was standing in front of the stands with his index finger up yelling number one. The other players went towards their respective parents hugging them with tears in their eyes. I looked for Tom and gave him a big hug and thanked him for his dedication. I then went to Sarah and squeezed her as hard as I could. I looked to my right and Tommy was crying in Dave's arms. I asked if he was ok and Dave replied, "He is happy." I looked to my left and Nathan was smothered by his family. Travis and David were hugging Jim and Ramona. I walked towards the blue line to get ready and just watched for a minute. Polly, Adam, and Johnny hugging Chewy. Sydnee was crying, holding her dad's leg with Pam holding her head. Jeff and his parents were hugging Caleb. CJ was hugging his mom and then skated to me and gave me one as he lined up ready to get his Medal.

The players lined up for their state champions medals. They announced Cadillac's team than ours. After each player received their medal we took a picture. I heard who they chose as the MVP and I quickly yelled to Brad to get up here so he could get a picture. Brad didn't know what was going on at first. He got a picture of Tyler receiving a plaque for MVP. Finally they announced the runner-up, Cadillac to come get their runner-up plaque. Then they announced our Polar Bears as State Champions. I told all the players go get your trophy. The players all grabbed at the plaque and held it high in the air.

The players were taking pictures with their plaque thanks to Michigan Hockey Weekly. I was approached by a nice gentleman named Jay Simon who asked for a quick interview with Michigan hockey weekly. Mr. Simon asked me how we did it. I just replied, "I told the kids you they are a good team, but to be a great team you have to work for it. This is about their work ethic. We are a third period team. The kids do all the work. All we do as coaches is blow the whistle." I left Mr. Simon with a handshake and off to take some pictures of my own.

The players took a few more pictures. Then it was time for our team photo followed by a photo with the entire Polar Bear family. I was thinking the whole time, "I couldn't believe that we did it." The kids never stopped believing and neither did I. Most of the parents were scrambling after the photos to get t-shirts, sweatshirts, and sweatpants with state champions on them.

We entered the bus and everyone sat down. I called for everyone's attention. I had a speech I had been planning for months. I said, "Players, I am proud of you for what you have done this season. I told you that you were a good team. Now you are a great team. Parents, thank you for your dedication. The last thing I have to say is there is a custom in championship hockey." I pulled the puck from my pocket and held it high in the air. "This puck always goes to the goalie." Chewy came up and took the puck from me with the biggest smile I had ever seen. I gave him a hug and George headed out of town playing "we are the champions", loudly on the radio.

We stayed the night in St. Ignace due to freezing rain. Kerry Roehm took care of everyone's rooms. After a short night we got back on the bus and drove to Newberry to drop off Gabriel and Warner. It was a tearful goodbye, but I was happy they came. We then took off for home.

As we got closer to Ironwood I sat on the bus and called each player to the empty seat next to me. One by one I told them how proud I was of them. I even called our student coaches, Jonny, Justin, and Jacob and personally thanked them for all of their dedication.

A few miles before we arrived in Ironwood I saw a Police car with sirens blazing escort us into town. There were a bunch of cars on the side of the highway taking pictures of the bus coming into town. We turned the corner and there were balloons and a gathering of people waiting for us to pull in. I got a little tear in my eye for all of the attention. George played, "We are the champions" one last time as we came to a stop and he opened the double doors.

The parents went out first then the coaches and with triumphant cheers the players were announced by Brian. The great support was astounding.

I was speechless and I needed a moment to give my mom a hug. I was surprised at all of the people that showed up. The support helped this team in more ways than I could count. Sarah and I got in the car and drove home.

Sarah and I took a moment to talk about the season. I needed her support to help me through the good times and the bad. This season was perfect. There wasn't anything negative and those 12 players gave every bit of blood, sweat, and tears they could all season long. I looked at the statistics we mustered as a team. Our penalty kill was at 96%, and our power play was at 54%. We had 16 shorthanded goals and we had 16 shutouts. It was amazing to me what each player did and how they contributed in every game. The players worked as hard in practice as they did in games.

A few weeks later, after the newspaper articles and internet blogging, we had our hockey banquet. Every team took their opportunity to talk about their team. When it was my turn I wanted to say so much, but I got a little choked up and had to finish my speech quickly. After the speech was done and the awards were handed out Brian had the players come and hoist their State Championship Banner to the roof. I was proud of them and I shed a tear.

It wasn't long after the banquet that the Squirts were asked to be Grand Marshals at the 4th of July parade in Bessemer, Michigan. Michigan Hockey Weekly's April's edition had the team with the caption "UP POWER". The following winter the squirts were Grand Marshals of the Jack Frost parade in December. The kids were getting the recognition they deserved.

In the spring I went to my cottage on Lake Superior. I took this time to reflect on the season. I started a fire and watched the sunset alone with my thoughts. A group of 12 players were as close as family could ever be. From the dedication of the coaches, parents, and community it was the combination that made it possible. Finally I thought to myself, "Thanks Mom & Dad that was for you."

I didn't know where the future would take these kids.

But what I did know is it would be perfect, Polar perfect.

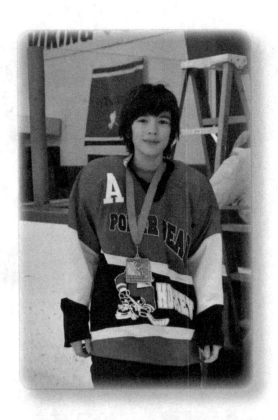

Printed in the United States
By Bookmasters